Rise Above the Sh**!

Down-to-earth thinking from Wisconsin

Rise Above the Sh**!

Down-to-earth thinking from Wisconsin

Mary Anne

Rise Above the Sh**
Down-to-earth thinking from Wisconsin

Published by Annie Press, LLC, a woman-owned company in Wisconsin, specializing in publishing materials with a purpose and promoting a "give-back" attitude. Charitable donations are given for every book sale.

Copyright © 2010 by Annie Press, LLC
All rights reserved, including the right of reproduction in whole or in part, in any form.

All book graphics and cover art by Nicole Brown, copyright © 2010 by Annie Press, LLC

Most Annie Press books are available at special quantity discounts for bulk purchase for fund-raising, events, sales promotions, and educational needs.

Please use our website, ANNIEPRESS.COM, for all inquiries, feedback, and requests.

DISCLAIMER: The author and publisher offer this book in hopes that the author's experiences and opinions inspire and enlighten; it is not based on any professional training of any kind. The author, publisher, and associates make no claims or guarantees and cannot be held responsible or liable for any results, actions or lack of actions, or damages or losses of any kind. In life, we are all responsible for our own choices.

Book Topics: Health, Mind, & Body, Life Enrichment, Personal Growth, Relationships, Wisconsin Author
ISBN-13: 978-0-9817983-0-1

Dedication

To my family and friends that supported me wholeheartedly, especially my kids, my sister, and my mom, who helped in any way they could.

To my honey, for allowing me to blabber out loud, at random, to think more clearly and formulate the words for this book. I am so grateful for your patience.

Thank you all for your endless, unwavering support in any crazy thing I might do. Thank you, God, for the people in my life, the inspiration, and for making everything possible. All of this helps me remember I can make my life everything I ever dreamed of!

Table of Contents

HOW TO GET THE MOST OUT OF THIS BOOK 1

INTRODUCTION 5

WHAT IS SH**, ANYWAY? 9

GRATITUDE ON A SMALL SCALE 13

I THINK THERE'S SOMETHING WRONG WITH ME 19

LEAVE THE SH** FROM THE PAST BEHIND 25

YOU WILL FEEL LIKE SH** IF YOU TRY TO HIDE BEHIND IT 29

WHY DO YOU PURPOSELY SET THE BAR LOW? 33

BE AMAZING BY NOT SHOWING OFF YOUR SH**! 37

WOE IS ME! 41

FEELING CRABBY? 43

SH** DISGUISED AS COMFORT 47

SH** WON'T MAKE YOU HAPPY! 51

DON'T DO SH** JUST BECAUSE SOMEONE ELSE DID 55

WORRYING DOES GET YOU SH** 59

I DON'T DESERVE IT 63

YOU ARE IN CONTROL 67

ARE YOU TELLING PEOPLE YOU'RE NOT WORTH A SH**? 83

DON'T SIT AND SPIN IN THE SH**! 87

NEED TO SHOW EVERYBODY YOU'RE AN IMPORTANT SH**? 91

DEMAND RESPECT? YOU'VE LOST IT! 95

DON'T ADD TO THE SH** PILE! 101

IF YOU CAN'T SAY SOMETHING NICE… 105

DID YOU GET LOST IN A RELATIONSHIP, SOMEWHERE? 111

YOU ALWAYS HURT THE ONES YOU LOVE 115

BE KIND! 121

PEOPLE ARE SUPPOSED TO HELP PEOPLE! 123

BIG PEOPLE ARE SUPPOSED TO TAKE CARE OF LITTLE PEOPLE 129

DO YOU HAVE ANY CHILDREN IN YOUR LIFE? 135

BELIEVE IN SOMETHING – NO WEAK EXCUSES ALLOWED 139

WHY ARE YOU AFRAID TO BELIEVE? 149

WHY AM I SO AFRAID OF MY SPIRITUALITY? 153

WHEN SH** COMES YOUR WAY, SIDE-STEP IT 157

SOMETIMES YOU NEED TO JUST SIT BACK, AND LET SH** GO! 161

LIFE WILL CHANGE—MAKE SURE YOU CHANGE FOR THE BETTER 167

SH** IS NOT ALWAYS AS IT SEEMS! 179

GRATITUDE ON A GRAND SCALE 183

DON'T WATCH OR LISTEN TO SH** 189

GET RID OF THE FRIGGEN STRESS OR THAT SH** WILL SNEAK UP ON YOU! 193

KNOW YOUR PRIORITIES 197

ARE YOU IN A FUNK? ARE YOU IN A RUT? STEP ONE IS TO ADMIT IT! 207

AREN'T YOU WORTH GIVING MORE TO YOURSELF THAN THE STANDARD CRAP WE SEE THESE DAYS? 211

YOUR LIFE DOESN'T HAVE TO BE THE NORMAL SH** 215

GOOD AND EVIL DOES EXIST 229

ARE YOU FOLLOWING YOUR DREAM? WHY NOT? 237

WHAT IS YOUR SELF IMAGE? 243

DON'T TREAT YOUR BODY LIKE SH**! 251

PUT A LITTLE EFFORT INTO YOU! 261

WHERE DO I BELONG? 273

THINK, PLAY, AND DREAM LIKE YOU DID AS A CHILD 279

FIND HARMONY! 283

DON'T HESITATE TO SHOW YOU CARE, APPRECIATE, OR LOVE 287

SAVOR! 291

TO WRAP IT ALL UP, IN A PRETTY, PLEASANT-SMELLING PACKAGE... 295

TALK TO ME! 299

HOW TO GET THE MOST OUT OF THIS BOOK

Will you get anything out of this book? Is it worth reading? I'll tell you right now that you will only get out of this, according to what you put into it. This book will do you no good if you do not want to think. You need to THINK! If you have an open mind and spend a few moments thinking through the ideas I present, you can get a lot out of it. I'm not saying you will share the same opinions I have; you may not at all. But if you allow yourself to escape the crazy-busy world for a few moments to think through how you really feel about the various topics, it will make picking this book up worth your while.

Take your time and just read through one short chapter at a time. Then take a break from reading on to the next chapter to allow yourself time after that to think about what you just read and about what your experiences have been. Think about how you really feel about it; whether you agree with everything I'm saying is not important. Just knowing how you feel about it is the mission! Most importantly, think about how you can change things to make your life better. Work on getting used to a new viewpoint or to the changes you want to make and take time to notice how it affects you in a good way.

Go back and read through it often to really let it sink in, so that it's natural for you. Practice your new, desired thinking as much as possible and again, re-read the chapter until it all comes natural to you. Then remember, even if you get it down, we all need reminders. Don't hesitate to take a few minutes every month or two and go back to read through at least some of the chapters you really liked again. It would make me feel much better to know the book has more purpose than just one read-through. Help me out :)

If you're a people person, the topics in this book are awesome for group discussion or conversation starters. Use it as an excuse to get together with your friends once a week or something! The more people, the more input and ideas you'll have to really dig in to the content! Some may even have recommendations on things that worked for them or for other books or information they've come across on the topic. A wise person will draw off of other people's experiences and apply it to help themselves.

I have one last wish for you. Since you're taking the time to read this book, you're taking time away from something else you could be doing. Make it really worthwhile and let your thoughts improve your life. Don't hold them back; you've done that long enough, probably. You'll be amazed how good it can be. Enjoy rising above, every day!

INTRODUCTION

This is NOT a read-once, that made-me-feel-good-for-the-moment kind of book. This is a read and re-read chapters until you have mastered it and it makes you feel great, long term. If you're serious about making your life all it can be, you'll keep this book nearby to help you think clearly when you need it most.

I was raised in the wide-open Wisconsin country, and try to keep my thinking the same—wide open. It is all too easy to get busy, get in a rut, get in a routine, and start imitating a robot—doing what you think you have to do, and what you think is acceptable to the majority. But with this pattern, we narrow our thinking to the point where life feels like a hamster wheel. That's NOT how it's supposed to be, and in a matter of seconds with clear thinking, you can jump off the wheel that goes no where and get moving on all your life is supposed to be. You just have to clear your head! It's so easy, you'll kick yourself for not doing it earlier in life, but no need; you still have plenty of life left to soar.

This book will give you some very short, simple starting points. I've tried not to lecture or personalize it too much, though I might tell you what definitely works for me at times. I feel I can get my points across best by being direct, so please don't be offended. I'm truly more interested in making a positive, long-term impact where I can, than seeking popularity or general acceptance. I don't ask you to bend to my way of thinking. I'm merely suggesting things that I feel fulfill my life, in hopes they work for others, too. I hope I am translating the clear thoughts in my mind to paper successfully, and that they benefit you, some how.

So, what's your deal?

Are you pretty content in life, but one of those "always looking to improve" kind of people?

-OR-

Are you feeling like you're stuck in a rut—same thing day in, day out and you would die for a break or a change?

-OR-

You don't want to believe this is all there is to life—you need a change right now, to maintain your sanity?

-OR-

Are you unhappy with where you are in life, or with the circumstances of your life, and need something new, now?

-OR-

Are you frustrated by some things people do and say, and just don't know what to do with them?

Whatever your deal, I'm hoping I can offer a word or two of advice to help you open up other options, or at least, put you in another place with a fresh perspective. Why am I the expert? Can't say that I am. I'm speaking only from my experiences or from the experiences of people that I have crossed paths with. Everything that works for me or them, may not work at all for you…but it also might.

Nonetheless, if you gain one thing that improves your life from this, it was worth the time you spent reading it, and worth the energy I've put into this. So, read on, and try out a new viewpoint, or if it's just not for you, leave it and make your own determinations. But for sure, take the pieces you think you could try and give it a whirl. What have you got to lose? Let it broaden your horizons in understanding others, but more importantly, in understanding yourself.

WHAT IS SH**, ANYWAY?

Actions, situations, and things that are not good for you equals SH.**

So, exactly what am I referring to when I say "SH**?"

Well, I guess I'm talking about the bad stuff—the negative stuff—in life. Mostly, though, the stuff that comes out of negative people. Think about any negative people you know for a second. Most people will avoid them, given the choice, as if they had an offensive smell to them. That's because they're splattered in SH**; sometimes, they're even covered in it. Unless you avoid them, they will get some of that nasty stuff on you, too. They dump their negativity, or their SH** on you too!

So what? Well, that tends to make you negative too, and thus, unpleasant for other people. If that's not who you want to be, you simply need to make some simple efforts towards rising above the SH** every chance you get. The easiest way to do this is to learn what you can from others. It gives you the jump-start of not having to try it out and wait for results yourself. Watch and learn from both positive people and negative people. Make a note to yourself about what works and what you absolutely should not do.

So, through the years, I've observed a lot of people, but have obviously tried some things out for myself as well. I find that it helps me to be reminded of some very basic things. It helps me to stay on-track. This book is my brain-dump of those simple things. You can take my ideas as I give them, change them some to meet your needs, or leave them behind completely. Do whatever you need to make your life everything you ever dreamed of.

It's important to identify all the SH** in your life, or in a particular situation. It's important to try to understand why others do the SH** they do. Identifying it helps you think clearly about what it is you are not satisfied with, and what you can do to change it. The chapters of this book talk about the SH** that I have noticed in at least one point of my life, or in other people's lives. I offer my view of what I think can help you change the SH**, should you desire.

Do I think I have all the answers? Hell, no! I'm just offering some of the things that became obvious to me, to someone I've observed, or to someone that I had a discussion with. Maybe you'll totally disagree with my way of thinking. Maybe my ideas would never work for you. That's okay. I'm not trying to brainwash anyone here, and let me point out that I don't have a lick of formal behavioral or psychology training. All I'm doing here is sharing some of my thoughts, along with some things that have worked for me or other people. It is meant to give you fresh perspectives, ideas, or more probable, just remind you of things you already know. My "mission" if you will, is to encourage you to take the time to think about who you are, and to emphasize that you are always in control of your thoughts and actions.

Those thoughts and actions are ultimately what determines how satisfied and fulfilled you are.

I bring up a variety of life topics that are in no particular order. You may have strong interests in some of these areas, and no interest in others. I suggest that if any of the topics are a source of any current grief, that you jump right to that chapter and begin there. My intentions are to give you ideas quickly on what you need most, today. Simply look at the table of contents and go to the topic you want.

I just ask you to remember that this book is merely my opinion. You are entitled to your opinion, too; so again, don't get stuck on something you don't agree with. You need to think through what makes your life good. You need to decide who you want to be. I can't be you. You can't be me. That's why we each need to do our own thinking and live our own life in whatever way is best for us. You owe it to yourself to be the beautifully unique person you were meant to be.

Just promise me one thing. Promise you'll let yourself think and spend nearly all of that time thinking only about what you want. Think big. Dream bigger. Live biggest of all!

GRATITUDE ON A SMALL SCALE

 **Don't forget how much you have. Appreciating it will bring you more.**

Sometimes when the world seems to rush by, we get caught in a trap of focusing on the negative. It's easy to do when you're tired physically, mentally, or emotionally. Everything seems to drag you down and you yearn for a change. Change is something you can initiate, anywhere, anytime, and I go into that in several other places in this book. For now, I want you to focus on being grateful.

Your life may be easy or it may be rough. Either way, I know you have several things to be grateful for. It's only healthy to stop and focus on the good things in your life, as often as you can. Did you hear that? It's only healthy. It will help you, trust me. These good things are always there, but we chose to ignore them. Sad, isn't it?

Take control of keeping yourself in perspective, no matter what's going on in your life. If you don't, you might as well crawl in a corner and stay there, and watch your life zoom right by. See, we worry so much about what's wrong in our lives; we don't take the time to enjoy what's right with our lives. It is a dirty, rotten shame!

So hang on, here we go! What do you have to be grateful for? Let's make a list. Bet at least a few of them fit you.

<u>I'll start with the big stuff.</u>

- You're either reading or listening to someone read this to you, right now. That means you're conscious, able to see or hear, and able to comprehend.

- You are not currently in a war zone, starvation zone, or disaster area, fighting for your life. (At least, not at this very moment, or you wouldn't have time to read this.) You are safe!

- You have the ability and the rights to acquire good reading material, such as this book.

- You or someone you know, knows how to read.

(You do realize that a good portion of this world does not have the simple life pleasures I just mentioned, don't you? How can you not feel blessed, when you're not lacking any of these basic things in life?)

<u>Now, move on to other things about you.</u>

- You try to be a good person and compliment the world, instead of sucking the life out of it. Give yourself a huge pat on the back for that. We need more like you!

- I'm guessing you are somewhat intelligent and are able to learn.

- Do you have food, shelter, and maybe even a job?

- Did you have enough money to buy this book? Some people don't, you know.

- You recognize that you can improve yourself and your life, or you wouldn't have bothered picking up this book. So many people will never come to terms with this, ever.

- What gifts or talents do you have? How are you different from other people?

- Be very grateful for any health you have; most people don't even think about this until something life threatening happens to them.

<u>Next, realize what's around you.</u>

- Are you fortunate enough to have anyone in your life that cares about you and your well-being? (Family, friends, coworkers, neighbors, associates.) Be thankful for each and every one of these people, and realize that the kinder you are, the more people you will have surrounding you.

- Do you have things beyond the basic necessities? Again, be grateful for each and every one of these things. Do you have somewhere to live? Do you get enough food to eat every day? Do you have clothing? What other possessions do you have or have the ability to have? Do you appreciate them? You probably have more than most of the people in this world, truly. The world goes beyond your neighborhood. Have you looked at the reality of a third-world country lately?

- What are you free to do? Can you choose where to live, where to work, what religion to practice? Any freedoms you have are a privilege that others literally die trying to obtain.

- What opportunities do you have to learn and improve your life, whether through other people, education, work, hobbies, etc? So many people in this world have none.

- Have you taken anytime to look at the environment around you? Both man-made structures and nature can be breath taking. Be happy you don't live in the rubble of a war zone, a flood zone, or a drought zone.

I'm sure I'm missed many more things that you have to be grateful for. Please add to your list accordingly.

Now that you're back in-tune with where you really stand in life, please keep it that way. Find a place in your daily routine to stop and remind yourself of the great things you have in life, and life's chaos will not be able to get a grip on you as often. There's a bonus, too. If you're occupying your mind with the good things in your life, you have less room in there to worry.

My personal method is to say my prayers and thank God for at least a few things in my life. My simple routine is to try to reflect on this whenever I have some quiet time, especially when I'm lying in bed, ready to fall asleep or ready to wake up, or anytime I'm alone. Another good place is anytime you're waiting, like in a waiting room, or while driving or riding somewhere. I'm sure we all have some of this. How about while you're taking a shower, getting dressed, or whatever? Find time, somewhere. It'll help you stay grounded all day and it just feels good. And yet another bonus: You automatically get the things you think about the most, so the more you appreciate anything, the more you get of the good stuff. Cool, huh?

I THINK THERE'S SOMETHING WRONG WITH ME

 **Seek out the beast within and kick some ass!**

Do you feel like you're just not always in control of yourself? Do you find yourself disappointed with how you act and react sometimes? Do you fight with yourself to go after what you want? Do you think that maybe there's something wrong with you? Well, join the club.

The reality is, every normal person has something "wrong" with them. Did you get that? Every single individual has something they themselves consider "wrong" with them. Well, gee, have you ever heard the phrase, "Nobody's perfect?" Where do you think that came from? Maybe from the fact and the reality that nobody is? Ya think? So don't worry so much about your goofy little SH**. Seriously.

I think that even if a person were raised from birth in a "perfect world" bubble, they would still not be "perfect." It's a natural fact. But it's a beautiful thing. How much character and personality would we each have, if things we experience in life didn't affect us? It molds us into what we are. No two people on this planet have exactly the same experiences, and thus, no two people turn out exactly the same. It gives us our beautiful uniqueness, faults along with the gifts. It's really very cool, if you think about it.

So why are faults or shortcomings good? Well, there's quite a few benefits. First, let's look at how it's good for the individual. If you know you aren't perfect, you are blessed with built-in modesty. You possibly have a desire to improve yourself or strive for higher things. You feel like you have conquered the world whenever you make it through one of your encounters with something you fear. You have compassion for others that struggle with the same fears, and it creates an automatic personal connection. The list goes on and on, but you need to realize that sometimes what you consider a "flaw" actually serves you. It can also serve others, especially if you have good intentions.

People need people. I'll lecture on this over and over, until people start listening! Our flaws, our fears, our lack and our needs force us to lean on others, at least now and then. Again, it creates natural personal connections as well as community connections. Not only are there other people around to help you with your inabilities, but you are there to help them, too. Isn't it a beautiful world? We were given everything we need, so long as people just acknowledge each other every now and then! I really believe this is key.

But maybe you say you've had enough of your blemishes and you don't want to expose others to them? That's fine, but don't burden other people by withdrawing from them. There is always something you can do to get your SH** together. What really helps me tackle something that I'm disappointed in, is to get to the root of the SH**. Often times, getting to the bottom of it will make it nearly disappear, instantly! I'm not exaggerating, either. Try it, you'll like it!

So how does one go about finding where all the crap begins? Take some time to think. I mean, really think. Find a quiet place or anywhere that you can hear yourself think. I love thinking through things while I'm lying in bed with my eyes closed, either just before I go to sleep, or right when I wake up. It's easier for me then because all the distractions of the day are not there. I can focus on ONE thing and give it all my attention. I keep a notepad by my bed for other things that pop in to my head—things I'm afraid I'll forget—so I write down the reminder and then I push the distraction out of my head. The notepad is also good for jotting down new ideas or things I might want to do to move towards something, or things I want to think through a little more. The worst to me is loosing a brilliant thought because I was half-awake. I have to admit, the majority of my inspirations hit me clearly during these times.

Once you have your quiet time to focus, bring out one thought of something that's bothering you. Did you react to something in a way that disappointed you? Are you fearful of something you don't want to be? Did something give you negative vibes or feelings? Okay, we need to find out why. The why is SO important! The "why" is going to help you move on. Actually, it's probably the only thing that's going to allow you to move on.

Fears, self-defeating actions, and insecurities, I think, come from a past experience or experiences. Somewhere, somehow, you had a negative feeling from something that happened in your past. You probably barely remember it, and you may have naturally suppressed it altogether. It could also be from something that didn't even happen to you, but something that you observed or heard about. So see, we can't just order a perfect world.

So ask yourself, why do I do that? Or why does that bother me? Now dig, and dig deep! Think back as far as you need to; very commonly, this is way back to when you were a kid. Allow yourself to try to remember the first time you felt that negative feeling, fear or insecurity, or whatever the feeling may be. The occurrence may be painful. It may be traumatic, so take it at your own pace. It may be the other extreme, though, where you barely remember, but nonetheless, it can affect you. Did you find it? Or find part of it? Good. That is huge!

Once you have some idea when it all started, ask yourself some questions and give yourself honest answers. And through it all, pound into your head that what happened in the past is done. It can no longer hurt you. It's over. Let it go. As soon as you do, it's as simple as that. It can't affect you anymore.

So if the negative feelings start up again, realize that something triggered it. Something made you refer to something in the past. That's fine; acknowledge the feeling was awakened. Then, remind yourself you don't want to feel that way anymore and that it's all in the past, so discard it and move away from it. React the way you really want to, not the way you had habitually responded before. And be forgiving to yourself! Although you're going to lick most of your "flaws" using this easy process, some may take more time or efforts. And don't be hard on yourself if once you have conquered it, the demon shows up somewhere down the road again. Keep it temporary, kick its ass, and move forward. Don't be discouraged and let it fool you into thinking you have lost. Don't let it lie to you and tell you that you can't do it. Take it day by day, in baby steps some days perhaps, but then leaps and bounds on the days you feel strong, all the while remembering why you need the change. Don't give up and you will kick its ass and leave the SH** in the past for good!

For those really tough things, realize you have endless resources to use to conquer and change it. If you want to keep it to yourself, check out all the books, internet information, or articles that may be around on the topic. Trust me, someone, somewhere has written about it in an effort to help other people through something they struggled with. Take what works for you and leave advice that doesn't work for you behind. Keep digging and don't give up. You will find something that works for you and you'll wonder why you didn't do it sooner. Don't get frustrated if you have to make adjustments and try again, or try a combination of what others recommend. Do what is best for you and go with what works for you. No one is exactly like you, remember?

If you're willing to share your "problem" with other people, remember, that's what people are for. Tough issues usually have support groups and organizations that can help, but friends (and sometimes complete strangers) can also utter a word or two sometimes that will resolve all your woes. Remember, when people give, it makes them feel great, so you're helping them too. It's not one-sided. Also remember, there are doctors trained to help people with the tough things. A good psychologist is often available with health insurance or a company employee assistance program that will pay the bill. And even if you have to pay out of your pocket, isn't your sanity and happiness worth paying a few bucks, if necessary? Once again, if the first person you seek out is not helping you, don't be discouraged. Keep looking and keep talking until you do find someone that can relate and offer advice that helps you. Never give up on yourself!

Whatever your imperfections, don't be so distorted to ever think you're the only one. You are extremely incorrect on that thought! Everybody has a past; everyone has fears, insecurities, or shortcomings of some type. It's normal and it's natural. But if people help people, guess what? It all works out. It brings us closer together and it defines us, so it's all good SH**.

LEAVE THE SH** FROM THE PAST BEHIND

 **Stop letting yesterday control your future.**

Eeks. Allowing crap from your past to alter what you're doing today has to be one of the biggest hurdles for the majority of the population! We can't help it. Without thinking, without knowing, we alter our behavior and hold ourselves back out of fear from past negative experiences or observations. Without knowing, we punish or deny ourselves at an extreme level!

And until you get to the bottom of it, to realize where it came from and how ridiculous it is to fear something from the past, you can't truly be and do what you really want to. It influences you, like I said, often without you even realizing it! Yes, negative things from your childhood to the present, whether you experienced them first-hand or watched or even heard about someone else's experience can hold you back. It can even be something as subtle as a less-than-wonderful feeling you had at one time, and the association of anything that occurred around that time, related or unrelated. And now you avoid something like the plaque just because it reminds you of that icky feeling. It's crazy how things get burned into our brains, based on feelings. Sometimes, it's okay, as we need to be informed, but only if it's not holding you back from what your heart really wants now.

So if you don't know you're letting your own demons get to you, how do you stop it? Well, start by stopping to think about something you're doing that is not exactly what you wanted. Ask yourself why you're doing it that way when it doesn't make you entirely happy. Ask yourself why you don't go after something you really want. Take some time to think through it, either by yourself quietly, or talk through it out loud with someone you can trust. Often times, other people can see things we are blind to.

As you find your way back to situations that may be causing your agony, resentment towards others involved may surface (or resurface). So blame them, perhaps for what happened, and acknowledge it as the source for your current shortcomings. Then, stop blaming them for your ability to do what you want, especially if it is completely in the past. Learn this about yourself, realize they may have been less than perfect, forgive, and forget!

What if you find it's someone in the present or a current situation that's messing with your heart? First, evaluate the root of the problem. Is there anything you are doing that might be causing or encouraging the problem? If someone in your life is making you miserable, have you tried everything to resolve it or avoid it? If you have and things are still bad, start making small changes about how it impacts you. For example, if you have to deal with a negative person that's dishonest and unreliable, don't let yourself get in a position where you have to trust them or rely on them. Have a backup plan. Then, when they jilt you, you can move on, unscathed, and just be grateful you would never treat anyone like that yourself.

What if you can't? What if the person causing your pain is a relative, parent, spouse, or child? Try different approaches and honesty. No good? Try distancing yourself, at least emotionally, from them. Whatever you do, don't push the SH** downhill! In other words, don't imitate their bad behavior and change who you are or who you want to be. And absolutely, don't take it out on another person, innocent or not. Deep down, acting negatively will never make you feel better.

Realize you deserve the chance of understanding yourself and what makes you happy, and what doesn't. Realize you deserve the chance to be happy. Realize the fears you are carrying along with you today cannot really affect what you're doing, unless you alter your behavior because of it. The past cannot harm you unless you choose to force it in the present to harm yourself. Does it make sense to harm yourself? Certainly not, so stop the battle! Leave the past behind, where it belongs, and promise yourself you will change. So getting to the bottom of the SH** is the first step; vowing to leave it behind and change your behavior is next.

How do you begin to change a habit you've been dragging around for so long? Take care of yourself so that all of your energy can go into changing things. Eat healthy, exercise, get plenty of regular sleep at night, and don't veg out too often. Seek out help! It's everywhere! If you're a private person, you can get help from the experts without anyone else having to know. Whether it's something you'd like to improve on or something someone else is doing that you'd like to understand, trust me, many others have gone through it and have defeated that demon.

The wonderful thing about that is, some of them took the time to write down how they won their battle and now, it's available to you! You can look for help on the topic in the library, a bookstore, or on the internet, and no one ever has to know. If you're comfortable enough to realize people only admire someone that looks to improve themselves, there's always support groups, friends or family that want to help. There are plenty of places to go. Try them all! The more you go after it, the quicker it will be in the past, forever!

Keep yourself going, even when you aren't actively working on your change with good, upbeat music. Let yourself sing out loud and dance, too. Music is one of the fastest mood setters ever! Appreciate every day and the fact that you are learning more about yourself and going after your bliss. Take the time to share your talents, time, and smiles. Let yourself take some chances, just to get some practice in realizing the past cannot harm you unless you invite it to do so. Feel the victory of conquering the monster of the past, feel the joy of really going after what you want, the way you want to!

YOU WILL FEEL LIKE SH** IF YOU TRY TO HIDE BEHIND IT

Don't use your issues as an excuse to attack others. You will be hit the hardest.

Very often in relationships, when we feel vulnerable, we spew sh* at the people we care about, which leaves us feeling super SH**TY. Why? Because it's easier than confronting the true issue. We hide behind the crap we throw out there and use it as a distraction. Most times, the distraction is for ourselves. We don't want to admit something is bothering us. We don't want to take the time to deal with it. We don't like confrontation. So, we spew SH** and make it worse. Not too smart, is it? Moreover, we push our SH** downhill, dumping it on the nearest innocent bystander and most likely, hurting and confusing them.

We don't want to think we're the problem so we try to convince ourselves and those around us, that it's their fault. Then we start picking at them for the dumbest things imaginable, that have nothing to do with what's bothering us. Guess it's a natural reaction when we feel hurt or afraid, but very often, it turns a little uncomfortable thing a into a very big issue. Moreover, it makes you really awful, along with hurting the very person you're probably struggling to be close to.

Let me give you a common example. Let's say you've been planning a special outing with someone you care about. You're looking forward to talking to this person, one-on-one, about some things you've been wanting to, for a long time. Then, as you're waiting to meet up with this person, they cancel on you for a very weak reason, like, they just don't feel like it. You try to talk them into it, but there's no changing their mind; they say they will reschedule with you soon. They don't want to chat on the phone long, and say they just want to relax at home. You are very disappointed and hurt that seeing you weren't more important to this person. You continue to feel hurt each time you chat with this person on the phone or through email, as they are not apologizing and seem to have forgotten all about it.

Your conversations with this person are now short, and you are irritable. You start to criticize them for something they did, totally unrelated. You continue to pick on them and withhold support for anything this person is doing, and maybe even pick a small argument. When this person tries to reschedule meeting up with you, you blow them off with a weak excuse, to try to teach them how it felt. What a mess!

Instead of just telling the person that they hurt your feelings, you turned ugly. They know something is bothering you, but probably don't have a clue that it's related to them. They probably just think you're trying to deal with something, and your moodiness is all because of that. With this assumption, they don't think they can be of any help and will probably try to avoid you, if they can, and wait until you're not crabby anymore. The SH** you threw at them has totally covered up the real issue. They can't possibly know what is bothering you, and may be changing their mind as to how they feel about you. Is that what you wanted?

My advice, that I wish I'd take for myself more often, is to shut the trap until you've had a chance to think about why you are upset with this person. Is it coming from something you're afraid of, versus the real, true issue that you really want to discuss? Maybe you don't even know what it is that's really bothering you, at first. Maybe all you know is you're feeling frustrated or anxious or worried. Try telling the person honestly, you feel "out of sorts" but you don't know exactly what's bothering you—just to give them a little warning. They might be able to help, though you shouldn't expect them to wave their magic wand and fix you instantly. Maybe they can't help at all and it's something you need to figure out, but it's still way better than being mean to them over something stupid and unrelated.

It's very simple. The more SH** you throw out there, the more it will build up between the two of you, sometimes even to the point where you can no longer get through it. Think it over and talk to each other honestly about the real problem instead of allowing fear to attack and blame. Things done out of fear will not make you or others feel an ounce of good, but you can't go wrong doing things out of caring, kindness, or love. Then, no matter the end result, you can feel good about it instead of feeling like sh*.

32

WHY DO YOU PURPOSELY SET THE BAR LOW?

Setting the bar low proclaims to the world that you have issues.

I think we're all guilty of this, to some degree. In some areas, more so than others. You sabotage yourself by setting the bar low, and actually think you're helping yourself. You may think you're protecting yourself. You may even think you're protecting others by thinking this way, as you can't disappoint them. Think it through. You're not helping yourself or anyone else. You're not sparing others any burden; you're actually causing more disappointment because of your lack of effort. It's disheartening to others.

Why do you purposely set low expectations in some areas of your life? Common areas, off the top of my head, are:

- Expressing feelings
- Giving others just "good enough"
- Accepting "good enough"
- Being reliable
- Staying healthy (getting exercise and eating only what we need)

- Not helping out as much as we should
- Not working as hard as we should

Why do you purposely lower the quality of your life and the quality of life of those impacted by it? You may think I'm being dramatic again, but think about it. Consider whether this is really what you want.

Look first at how others perceive you. Maybe it's easiest for you to think of someone else that has set the bar low in one of these areas. Let's say, someone that's overweight. Honestly, what are your first thoughts about them? They must be lazy. They must have some mental issues smoldering that causes them not to take care of themselves. They could be so much more attractive without all that extra weight. Right? Be honest.

So guess what? If you think this of someone else, people also think the same of you, if you're at all unhealthy, whether it's too much weight or scary skinny. You don't have to be 100 pounds overweight. Even a little chubby makes people think this way. Your body is the only one you get for this lifetime, so if you're not taking care of it, you're hurting your future, so people assume you must have issues. Let's look at another example.

What do you think of people that seem to be afraid to express positive feelings towards others? Maybe you once dated such a person, or have a friend or even a significant other that holds back their feelings. Again, what's your honest judgment of this person? They're insecure or afraid to show their feelings. Something hurtful in their past has damaged them. They miss out on the really good relationships because of it. They are maybe a cold, heartless person. It's hopeless to expect anything more of them—they will always be miserable. They're messed up for life. You may even think they just don't care and aren't worthy of your care.

Harsh? Maybe so, but all so true, isn't it? So guess what? When you set your bar low, thinking you're so smart and keeping people's expectations of you where they belong, you are giving them a horrible image of you that I bet you really didn't want to. You're not protecting yourself from them asking too much of you. You're pushing them away by making them think you have too many issues of your own already that you can't handle. They may become angry with you, feel sorry for you, try to help you, and many times, they will give up on you. Is that REALLY what you wanted?

This hurts the most in personal relationships, when feelings aren't expressed as much as they should be, or where lending a hand isn't offered as much as it should be. The receiver of your "low expectations" can't help but feel like you don't care about them. The natural reaction is to stop caring about you, because they can draw no other conclusion other than you need to deal with your own problems before you can be a loving, giving person. At first, they'll have to begin balancing the relationship by withholding their feelings and expectations, and not helping you out too much when you need a hand. But eventually, they'll grow tired of the "dead" relationship and yearn to move on, and leave you behind to deal with your insecurities and personal demons.

Is that REALLY what you wanted? Assuming it's not, I have great news for you! It only takes a tiny bit of change to make a big impact and to begin raising your bar. Any little positive thing you do will be recognized and appreciated a great amount by someone. And there's a bonus! YOU will feel incredibly gratified by it. So maybe even do it just for you. After all, you need to care about yourself and take care of yourself to be the best to others. All it takes is one little change at a time. Or just go for it and make some big changes before it's too late. But watch out; people might think you've lost it. Ahh, but as long as you make them smile, does it matter?

BE AMAZING BY NOT SHOWING OFF YOUR SH**!

 **Even the most tolerant people will avoid a pity party.**

Just when I think I had seen it all, someone amazes me. I can't believe the strength I've seen in people, as they're going through a tragedy, they lose a loved one, or get news they have a deadly disease, and yet, there they are, smiling and being positive, and making others feel good! Oh, we all know they have to be all torn up inside, and hurting an unbelievable amount, yet there they are, consoling, even uplifting, everybody else. They don't feel sorry for themselves. Unreal, isn't it? I admire and respect these people so much, and only hope that some day I have a little bit of the positive impact they have on others.

Then you have the other side of the world. The people that amaze me by drumming up constant drama and showing off the yucky SH** they have, in a sad, sad effort to get attention. What happened to these people? Is it a brain chemical malfunction? Are they just horribly insecure? Are they still looking for that attention they feel they never got from a parental figure? I think they honestly think that if they make people feel sorry for them, they are locking people in, somehow. How messed up is that? Yet, just try to tell me you don't know some people like this. Seems to be more and more common. Depressing, isn't it?

And the really depressing thing is that these people don't realize that instead of guilting people into being around them, they are pushing people away. Once someone realizes they're dealing with a drama queen or a constant complainer, they will do their best to avoid them. People know that these types of people will only bring them down, and any healthy person does not want to be brought down. People like to feel good and be uplifted, not feel like someone tied an anchor to their ankles and threw them off a bridge! Yikes!

Now sometimes there is a medical reason for this behavior, like depression, for example. So here, I'm talking about the more common, non-medical, just-need-a-kick-in-the-butt behavior. You know the kind. They're always complaining about someone or something in their life that is not right. It's always someone or something else's fault that they are not happy, and that their life is awful. People avoid them as much as possible, because often, a confrontation leads to fighting, crying, or some other negative, embarrassing incident.

These sad saps haven't apparently thought through what other people really think of them, or they'd stop the madness, immediately. They also haven't thought about how we are all equal, from our uniqueness and importance in the world, to our responsibility and control over some of our emotions. Don't they think that it'd be just as easy for the rest of us to go psycho, every time something wasn't quite right in our lives? Do they really think life is easier for us, and that we were born with more willpower? Again, messed- up thinking for a messed-up individual. So sad and so changeable!

All the pathetic person needs to do is start making some choices to feel better about themselves and make the decision that they WANT good things and they WANT to be happy. Happy, brain-healthy people have no desire to rip on other people, dwell on the negative, or bring other people down. So I challenge the whiners to take a good, hard look at what they're doing and who they really want to be. It's never too late. Perhaps my honest brutality will help initiate the change, so for all the constant complainers out there, here goes. If I feel there's no hope for this type of person, I steer clear of them because I don't want the negative influence from them. If there's a chance this person could improve and be fun, though, occasionally when I'm in a really good mood and know they won't be able to bring me down, I might go out with them, just to see if they've changed their ways. If they have, I make more of an effort to hang around them. If they haven't, I make a mental note to always be too busy when they call, to be kind. So see, trying to guilt someone into hanging around a whiner never works. Us happy people will run like hell!

WOE IS ME!

People run from compulsive complainers because they know they have issues and don't want to fix them.

Oh! Ohhh! Ohhhhh! Oh, shut up already! (Don't you just feel like saying this to some people, sometimes?) We all know somebody like this, where something is always wrong. This person is almost always sad or crabby. I hope for your sake, this is not a description of you, but if it is you, you might want to read this chapter extra close. Maybe even read it twice?!

Some people throw their own pity party. Sadly enough, usually on a daily basis. They practice their sad face until it becomes so routine for them they fear something is wrong if they accidentally smile! But fear not, the second they realize they took their sad face off, they'll slam it back on again.

Now in my defense, I am not a heartless being. Please continue reading! I'll be the first to admit, I don't understand this type of person. Are they waiting for someone to tell them how rough they have it? Are they waiting for someone to rescue them? Why?

Obviously, they don't understand that it's only natural for others to want to avoid them like the plague! I mean, think about it. If you see a high pile of soupy crap oozing towards you, do you jump in it? Are you drawn to it? Hell no! You do your best to carefully step around it, back away from it, or if it's coming fast enough, you make a run for it. So why do these people think they can entice people to want to be around them? Sad. Obviously, they didn't really think it through.

Now I'm not saying these people don't have reasons to be down. They probably do, but who the hell doesn't? Everybody has some bad stuff in their life, past and present. This is what the "woe is me" person has forgotten. And for Pete's sake, it's not a competition! You tell me, what is the prize if you life is crappier than somebody else's? Yea. That's my point.

Everybody goes through hard times, bad things, and unforeseen events in their life. It's not just a special few that have the right to complain. Everyone has something they could complain about. The wise man, however, knows that constantly sharing their SH** and whining doesn't make it any better. Oh, contraire! It will almost always make it worse. In addition, the crap will just keep piling on and seeping out and cause the whiner more pain.

You can't blame people for alienating them. I mean, you try to bring them back to a better perspective, but when they fight you all the way and pull away from you to go sit right in the center of the crap pile, what can you do, but to leave them there to sink in deeper, all alone? And alone they will be, until they come to the reality that everyone has rough things in their life, and someone absolutely DOES have it worse than they do, but even so, there is no prize or reward of any kind, for wallowing in your own giant pile of poop.

FEELING CRABBY?

You let yourself and others down when you're not the real you.

Okay everybody, here's the reality. We all feel a little crabby every once in a while. It happens. You're human. So don't feel bad about it. Do yourself a favor though. Get to the bottom of it and get over it. Everyone else will appreciate it too. I mean, does anybody really want to be around a crabby person? Absolutely not! People will run, if they can. Wouldn't you?

What do I mean by get to the bottom of it? Just that. Think about why something's irritating you and what you can do about it. You are always in control of how you respond to something. You are always in control of whether you let something make you crabby or whether you let it go.

Here's some advice you may have heard before: If you can control it, work towards a solution and be content knowing things are getting better. If you can't control it, let it go! While you can't always ignore it, you can choose to not let it bother you. Really, you can. Maybe you can't always stop it from making you crabby, temporarily, but the thing to conquer first and foremost, is to keep it temporary! Deal with why it's bothering you, and how you're going to change your reaction to not let it bother you any longer. Face it, and let it go. I'll give you a personal example.

One of my pet peeves has always been lazy coworkers. It used to really stress me out and change my behavior for the worst. It made me crabby and short on patience. I hate acting like that, so it made me even crabbier! I finally realized why it made me crabby. Past experiences were reminding me that when others didn't do their share, I'd end up with more work. I'd end up having to clean up a disorganized mess that I hadn't created. My coworker's shortcomings would make me and my company look bad. It wasn't fair. On top of that, it might affect my raises or job opportunities in my future. It really urked me.

When this occurred, I'd succeed in relieving the stress (and crabbiness right along with it) by just remembering the truths about the situation. First of all, lazy coworkers made me look good. Not only did I know I was doing a going job, but it would be obvious to everyone else that I was doing a great job, by comparing my work to my peer's. When it came time for reviews, promotions, or lay-offs, this would be a factor if I was working for anyone that mattered. If this management was worth working for, they would recognize my efforts and reward me accordingly. This was enough to motivate me to continue working there, despite what people around me were doing. Some managers and companies are not worth working for, though. I say that because even despite hard work, sometimes people are not treated fairly. When this occurs, it's a flashing neon sign that you are not working for the right people and you need to look for other opportunities. Working hard for people that don't appreciate it is a waste of time;

open yourself up to new ideas, careers, or locations. Remember, you are in control of how you choose to make the money to pay your bills, just as you are in control of the rest of the things in your life. I appreciate all the negative situations in past jobs that forced me to start looking for another job. It always advanced me in every way, and instantly resolved the irritation!

Getting back to irritations we sometimes have. Don't waste time being crabby, instead, think through the facts and the truths about why it's bothering you, and often, that in itself will be enough to get you back to the mood you really wanted to be in. If not, make a commitment to yourself to change something to relieve the situation, whatever or whoever it may be, and to just do what is really best for you. You will feel back in control of yourself and avoid any regretful behavior because of it.

SH** DISGUISED AS COMFORT

Your comfort-seeking habits may be hurting you, and others.

If you are a human being, you most likely have a "comfort escape" or two. That's okay—we all deserve this. Babies often fill this need by sucking on their thumb; just because we're not babies anymore, the need for comfort doesn't just go away. So we resort to all kinds of things to temporarily escape, comfort ourselves, or just reward ourselves. There's nothing wrong with that and everybody's different. We all find soothing in different ways.

The key to contentment here is to make sure it's really giving you want you needed. Is it healthy? Is it positive for you and those around you? Does it REALLY make you feel better, in the end? Whenever you find yourself seeking that escape, keep the well-known phrase, "everything in moderation" in the front of your brain to give yourself a fair chance to achieve the good feeling you're yearning for. Don't allow your plan to backfire.

Food. Alcohol, caffeine, nicotine, or drug highs. Shopping. Gambling. Casual Sex. Vegging out to TV, video games, constant texting, or the internet. Sleeping an extreme amount of hours, unnecessarily.
Abandoning the people we are responsible to and hiding

out somewhere, whether it's a room in our home, the outdoors, or any other location. These are just some of the common ways people escape or look for comfort. We each have our personal preferences and may not even be aware of how we use these things and what we're trying to accomplish. If you ever find yourself looking back shortly after in regret, asking yourself, "Why did I do that?" or "Why didn't I just stop myself?" you were not happy with the outcome. So, learn from it and strive to think it through and control it, next time.

For example, I noticed that when I was really stressed out at work or with my relationships, I had the urge to chew on something constantly. Gum didn't do it—I wanted more texture. I found myself polishing off sweets, chips, crackers, or whatever was handy, by the boxful. When it didn't satisfy me, I rummaged for something more, knowing there was no one "fix." Later on, when I started to relax and realize my gut was about to explode, I was so disappointed with myself. Not only was it unhealthy, but it was in the opposite direction of my goal to not gain weight. Why did I just do that?

It was obvious that when I was anxious in a negative way, I went searching for comfort in food. Rarely was I ever hungry, either when I started out or when I went back for seconds, thirds, fourths, etc. I just wanted the escape. Merely realizing this has helped me a tremendous amount. While I'm no where near perfect and still fall sometimes, I am usually very aware of what I'm doing and try to deter myself in any way I can. Sometimes I make myself stay away from the food and try chewing viciously on a half a pack of gum. Sometimes I try to fill myself up with water or quickly go make myself do something else to keep me away from the food. If I have time, I head outside for a walk, vowing to put off the urge and reconsider once I'm back. Because walking relaxes me, the urge is completely gone by the time I return. But as a backup, I keep healthy options available, like carrots or somewhat healthy crackers. Anything but chips and sweets. Again, far from perfect, as I still give in sometimes, but then I try to watch the quantity. I try to think of the outcome before I fall into the behavior, and I quickly remember that overindulging only leaves me feeling rotten. Trust me, it helps!

Also, it's no secret that people will use drug- or alcohol-induced highs, including caffeine and nicotine, as an escape. I'm not telling anybody they can't touch this stuff, I'm just asking you to stop and think before you begin. Keep an emotional healthy control over it. Realize why you want to engage in the behavior and what the outcome will be, before you indulge. Make sure it's really what you desired. If it's not, admit to yourself it will not help and choose a different option. You DO have the right to choose your own options. Remember that. If you still decide to go ahead, set a limit for yourself beforehand—anything that works for you. Set either a quantity or a time limit, or better yet, the level of buzz you plan to achieve. Once you've hit the preset limit, make sure you have a strong plan to stop or taper off. Drinking until I'm hammered and spending the whole next day feeling like a truck ran over me doesn't accomplish anything for me. I doubt it helps you out at all, either. I doubt it provides the level of contentment you were going for. So, if you're going to drink, know why you're doing it, then pace yourself and keep yourself in check, and finally be in control to stop when you want to. Feel free to have someone you can trust help you out here; regardless of their feeling on the topic, a true friend will help you out, just because it's what you asked them to do. Sometimes a subtle reminder is all it takes.

Again, I'm not Miss Goody-Goody, trying to tell you to never touch anything that gives you comfort! I'm just asking you to stop and think first, before overindulging, and be honest as to whether it REALLY provides the permanent comfort you're looking for. If it's not, start by admitting it to yourself and by planning to limit it, or remove the unhealthy behavior altogether. Then, say when or change the behavior altogether, and give yourself a major pat on the back. Every time you do this, you can smile. You are moving closer towards contentment.

SH** WON'T MAKE YOU HAPPY!

 **Fulfillment comes from the inside-out, not the outside stuff**

Wanna be happy? I mean really, really happy? Don't go looking for it in the wrong places. The wrong places are things that provide instant gratification, but can't go any deeper than that. They can't fill the innermost longings of your heart.

Be careful that if you do have or do desire, any of these shallow sources of "bliss" that you don't make them a priority in your life. Be honest with yourself about what these things can or cannot provide. Let me explain a little more with some examples.

Money. Sure, we all gotta have it for the basic necessities, but thinking it's one of the most important things to have will make you miserable. If you are a greedy person, no amount will ever be enough.

Other material things, like properties, cars, clothes, etc. Keeping up with the Joneses is a sad, sad epidemic. These people shout to the world, "I have no worth as a human being, so I must hide behind my possessions!" Sadly, most of these people will never find their way out of the massive debt they create, let alone, ever find their self-worth.

People. Before you throw your arms up on this one, let me explain. I sincerely believe the world revolves as it should when people are there for each other. I just think some people have the wrong idea, thinking they aren't responsible for their own happiness and well-being. Instead of focusing on what would make them feel good about themselves, they wade in their misery as they wait for "that special someone" to appear and magically change their life and make them happy. There's also the people that blame their unhappiness on someone else. The truth is, no matter who is, or who is not, in our life, you are still the only person that can ultimately control your satisfaction in life.

Addictions. You may think this doesn't apply to you, but hear me out as I move in to the non-obvious addictions in a minute. Most of us are guilty of having some type of addiction. I ask you to keep an open mind here, and be honest with yourself as I go through these. For this purpose, I'm defining addiction as something you just feel like you have to have, and are unhappy without it. It has some control over your mood, and without it, you struggle in trying to change your mood in a positive way. Do you see how dangerous this is?

First, let's talk about the obvious addictions—substances. There's the hard-core ones, like alcohol and drugs (both legal and illegal; it doesn't matter when you're talking addiction). But there's others too, like food, soda or coffee, sweets, and anything else you don't have full control over. If it affects your mood, it's an addiction.

Second, and probably more common, are behavioral addictions. These can be all over the board, so I'll give you some examples. Some people need to spend money when they're low. Some people need to whine to someone, every time they're stressed, or agitated, or sense an injustice. A lot of people have an "escape" addiction. This is a place or activity you run to anytime you feel anxious or stressed. Some people crash in their bed or on their sofa and sleep for hours. Some veg out, watching meaningless TV. Some get the munchies and have to chew on something. Some blow off family functions or commitments they had, sometimes including work. Some go fishing. Some work out. Some bury themselves in work. Some drive off to nowhere. Some look for attention from strangers and sleep around. I bet you can think of a few more behaviors that you've observed, or maybe have done yourself. No matter what it is, it serves the same purpose—to escape in an effort to change your mood.

I think you get my point, but let me reiterate. I'm not saying that if you partake in any of these things, that it's bad. I'm simply saying that if you're using one of these things routinely as a means to feel fulfilled, you may be avoiding the one thing, the only thing, that will bring you ultimate peace.

This one thing, the only thing you have full control over, is you. Based on everything I've tried and have witnessed in other people in my 40-plus years of life, self-fulfillment and real happiness comes from the inside-out. Start with doing things that you are proud of, so that you are a positive influence on the world, and you'll learn who you really are and what makes you happy.

Addictions are surface things; they lie on the surface but they are not a part of you. They may give you a few moments of fun or escape, but it's only a coating that wears away all too quickly. Because it never provided anything to your core, once it's gone, you feel empty and you long to find a way to fill the void.

If you look it up in a dictionary, you'll see different definitions of the word, fulfill, yet they all point to the same thing, like "complete" or "satisfy." Some even say, "As a duty or prophecy." Interesting, isn't it? The actual definition to me strongly implies that fulfillment comes from us carrying out our destiny, or becoming the person we were meant to be.

So there you have it. Wash away all of the SH** that affects you or those around you negatively so you can be the person you were born to be, and you'll be pleasantly surprised by the strong and in-control person that's been dying to come out. Only then will you find inner peace and fulfillment in life.

DON'T DO SH** JUST BECAUSE SOMEONE ELSE DID

Think about how you want to be and do it, no matter what you've seen, heard, or learned earlier.

One of the first keys to contentment is doing things because you want to. I mean you *really* want to. Whether you do it for yourself or someone else, you need to be in control of your actions. This means you should NEVER do something just because someone else did, someone else thinks you should, or because everybody else is doing it. Stop and think first. Is it what you really want to do, and are you comfortable with it?

The most obvious piece of this is something most of us heard growing up, "If somebody else jumped off a cliff, are you going to, too?" Our parents weren't just spouting off. They were trying to get us to think. We thought it was a dumb thing to say, but now we realize they were trying to help us. You should know by now that real people and real friends don't just like you for following whatever they do. They like you for thinking on your own, and for the unique person you are. If you have friends that diss you because you don't go along with what they're doing, I want you to think. Are they really a friend or a robot-controller? In that case, you are the robot!

This especially applies to doing something bad, wrong, or negative. Be careful of those yucky people that will pressure you an immense amount to get you to do something wrong they are doing. They are not cornering you for your own good, but to try to convince themselves that they're not the only "bad" person. Misery loves company, you know. Don't let them suck you in to their SH** pit.

Now here's the piece most of us don't stop and consider at all. Are you doing something just because you observed it growing up? The biggest one here is imitating a habit or behavior that a parent or other adult might have done, or even an older sibling, relative or friend. There's some big, bad ones here, people. Drinking, smoking, how we raise our own kids (yeah, right down to things we say to our kids), but also abuse!

Or maybe it's not someone for the past, maybe it's someone you're presently observing. Perhaps you're just imitating everyone around you now, because it's a new situation for you and you think it's what you should do. That's fine, if it's truly the best thing for you and others, but please, take the time to think about it first, or here's a light example of what can happen. My city cousin came to visit me on the farm when I was a little girl. She had never walked through a barn or a cow yard before I took her on an adventure to show her around there. She followed me, careful to stay close behind, right up to the wooden gate I started to climb over. Once I was standing on the other side, I was confused why she remained standing on the other side, with no movement towards the gate. Turned out her shadowing me got her a mouth- and nose-full of cow manure, as I lifted my messy foot over the gate! Don't end up with a face-full, just because you didn't apply thought and logic to what you should be doing versus what someone around you is doing!

It's scary, but it's been proven. A lot of our behavior comes from merely imitating someone we observed, good or bad. But here's the catch. You are still the one that decides which of these behaviors you will do, only because you want to. If you are doing anything just because someone else did, really be honest with yourself if that's how you want to be. If not, decide right here and now, that you don't want to do it anymore and YOU CAN STOP! You can break the pattern! You need to do it for you, and for everyone around you. Especially anyone that may be watching you and will imitate you, down the road!

Don't feel bad. It's only natural for us to imitate those that raised us or those that impress us somehow. It's not because you're weak or anything. It's just human instinct. Hopefully you picked up some good behaviors too, and feel free to imitate the crap out of them! This goes for the present, too. If you see other good behaviors, don't hesitate for a second to copy them. Somebody might even see you do it and want to copy you, too! So now, it transitions from you spreading a negative domino effect to a positive domino effect. Pat yourself on the back!

True fulfillment comes from doing what you know is right for you and for those around you, as well. Discontent and misery comes from doing things you really don't want to be doing, regardless of whether someone's pressuring you into it, or if you just imitated it from someone else. You are not that other person. You are YOU, and the world is waiting for you to find yourself. Cut free and just be you.

WORRYING DOES GET YOU SH**

Worry can actually cause the opposite of what you want to happen.

Worry. It's an evil animal, and very hard to conquer sometimes. I recommend that you throw worry away for good. It serves no purpose, other than to make you and those around you miserable. If you can think of a positive effect that you get from worry, well then, worry away, but I bet you can't think of any!

Oh, I'm not saying you shouldn't care. You should. Just don't confuse caring with worrying. When you care, you can take all the precautions you should to set things up for the best outcome. Then, you should reassure yourself that you've done everything you could and don't worry.

Sometimes you have no control over things or people, and all you can do is hope and pray that things will work out for the best. I'll emphasize the pray, in case you're really serious about it. I'll tell you what, it works for me; many, many others have told me it works for them. And there's a bonus! You can even pray that you stop worrying, so it'll make you feel better, all around.

All over in this book, I emphasize that whatever you think about the most, you get more of. It does not matter whether it's a good thing or a bad thing. It does not matter whether it's something you want or something you don't want. There is nothing sorting out what you want, from what you don't want. Whatever you think about the most in any form, will become your reality. Your free will, through the contents of your thoughts, is the most powerful influence on your future. God made it that way, to give us the gift to choose who we want to be and how we want our life to be. Good or bad, He lets us choose.

The more thoughts that go toward something, the more likely it is to become reality. This includes thoughts from anyone and everyone. As the number of requestors increases, so does the power of the request. In addition, the energy and priority of the thought fuels the power of the request, and so, the more often that thought occurs, the faster it will become reality.

So think about the harm that can be caused by discussing something you or someone else doesn't want, over and over, day after day, to a variety of people, who go out and continue discussing it with others. You are all summoning what you didn't want through your worrying! The quantity and magnitude of the thought is bound to make it happen! Yikes!

The solution? Do not discuss, or even think about, what you don't want, ever! Talk about what you do want. Place the focus on the exact opposite of what you do not want.

Here are some examples:

Instead of Thinking or Discussing	**Think About or Communicate This**
Details of an injury or illness	Healing options, prayers for healing, appreciation for what you have, future healthy activities
Missing a deadline or opportunity	Options to be successful, re-prioritizing, feelings of accomplishment and the events that follow the success, gratitude
The worst that could happen	The best outcome possible, even if you're not sure what that is.
How someone is letting you down	Things you appreciate about that person, things that might help that person
Anything you're uneasy about	Pray for the best outcome for everyone, and remind people to pray as there is power in quantity and intensity

Most of all, you must believe. Trust that God has blessed us with the power to create our own lives through our thoughts. "Ask and ye shall receive." Of your thoughts, prayer can be the most powerful, if you focus on it often, in a positive way, and with great effort. Again, quantity helps, so don't hesitate to ask people to pray for what you want. In the very least, it can help them replace any negative thoughts about it and keep the wrong requests away.

Don't waste a moment worrying that people will think you're in denial or not being realistic. Reality is a matter of opinion and free will. Someone else's reality does not need to be your reality. You are the owner of your thoughts, and thus, your life. Wanting and asking for the best doesn't hurt anything, but worrying about what you don't want can bring the world down on you, in an instant. Remind people that worrying doesn't do anyone any good and that you need their prayers and positive thoughts to help out. More importantly, remind yourself so that deep in the back of your brain, you understand that you can just ask God to take over for you, and keep you strong and positive. Go about your day, making it the best day possible, trusting that God is there to help carry whatever we need Him to. Miracles do happen, every day, but not without the effort of the determined thoughts, the prayers, and the belief. You get to choose, but for me, it's a no-brainer.

I DON'T DESERVE IT

Simply thinking it through and making simple changes will help you feel deserving of everything good.

I didn't know where to start on this topic because honestly, I feel like I have a lot of self-training left on it. Seems like I have to constantly remind myself and argue with myself to go after what I want, and to not let great things and people pass by me in life. That I deserve it all! I know I do, because each and every one of us does. It's one of the reasons we are here—to gather all that is good. So why the struggle?

As always, I can only analyze where my thinking comes from, but I think it's a pretty common thought. Many of us view modesty and humility as great traits to have, and we admire people that possess them. I certainly do, but recognize that it's only healthy to the degree that it doesn't infringe on your self-confidence or towards your thinking on what you deserve, so there's definitely more to it.

Growing up, many of us were taught that you had to work hard, maybe even sacrifice and suffer, to get the really great things in life. You had to earn it. Many think this is the only way to obtain heaven after we die. Moreover, if things are too easy, or too good to be true, something bad was probably coming because you didn't deserve all of this. Worse, if you made things too easy in this life, heaven would be unobtainable. We think that you have to suffer in one place or the other. I know this is not how God meant it to be, so I think we've over thought this one too much.

God wants good. He wants us to feel good and be happy. Truly happy, right down to our soul. He wants ultimate bliss for us, in other words, heaven. I know that my deep-down happiness comes from feeling like I'm doing all I can to be a good person and do good in this world. Sometimes it means pushing myself to not be lazy and re-prioritize sometimes, temporarily, to do something for someone else. So is this sacrifice? Not really. It's just re-prioritizing. Maybe I re-prioritize at the expense of not doing something or getting something I wanted to, but I wouldn't call it sacrifice because I still get way more out of it, than I'm giving. In addition, it may open my eyes to how worthless the item or event that I gave up really was. So in my mind, it's really not a sacrifice, or something I have to "lose" to gain. Not if you look at the deep-down result it has on me.

So when we don't follow our heart completely and do good, do we deserve great things? Maybe, maybe not. We are our own judge of that. So maybe when we think we don't deserve something, it's because we don't feel we are the best person we can be? Maybe we're hard on ourselves for those times we are lazy, judgmental, self-serving, or demonstrate any other negative behavior? Maybe we deserve only as much as we give out? Maybe so. It's your own internal judge that you have to deal with, and if this is what's making you feel insufficient, well, it's easy to change. Immediately. Just remember, we are all human and thus, not perfect. God forgives us constantly, so we should too. God tells us that no matter who we were yesterday, or what we have done in the past, He will always forgive you and always wants you to be happy. No matter what you did! Your behavior today, from this moment on, is what counts, not what you did in the past. Learn from the past mistakes and regrets and then leave them behind (please read the section, "Leave the SH** from the Past Behind," in this book)! Say you are sorry and know that you will be a better person from now on, and you will slowly remember that you do deserve all good things and a great life. Follow your conscience. Even the smallest gesture or act of kindness, or even a smile when you aren't really in the mood will make you feel better.

I do value modesty and humility as respectful traits to have, but only to the point where you aren't keeping yourself from enjoying what you do deserve. If you do your best to do good, you shouldn't keep yourself from enjoying all the great things life has to offer. Again, God's desire is for us to live in a state of bliss. We define our bliss. So make sure any negative influences from your past or from others doesn't keep you from it. Remember to use your own heart to think about, and quickly discard the following statements, for good. I am most certain these weren't part of God's design for our happiness:

- Anything that's too good to be true, usually is.
- I'm not good enough.
- I have to go through hardship to get the good.
- If I'm happy in this life, I will pay for it in the next.

It's all a bunch of crap, as it does not logically fit into God's plan of allowing heaven to exist in the present and providing an abundance of everything that is good. I will admit that we should do our best to help others and treat them with respect and likewise, behave in a way that respects our own body and soul completely to feel worthy of all we have at our fingertips. I think it helps us to feel like we do deserve things, and thus to enjoy them more. But I think we need to keep a good balance and allow ourselves good things, instead of pushing them away because of past or present negative thoughts.

Don't ever be afraid to focus on how you want to be and what you want in your life, deep down in your heart. Follow what makes you feel GOOD. Do anything you can to make up for things you neglected in the past, work on being a better person, and then, don't hesitate to pursue your dreams and feel like you deserve them. Today is what matters to your internal judge. What you do from now on determines your level of happiness, and what you feel you deserve.

YOU ARE IN CONTROL

Only you choose how something impacts you, what you want, and what choices you make. You are completely responsible for you and your entire life.

You are in control of your life. You are solely and completely responsible for you. It's time to get rid of the crap you've been blaming things on and start living a real life. You wanna blame someone? Blame you. Blame yourself for not loving and respecting yourself enough to be who you should be. It's time to peel off the layer of crap you are dragging around and to get to the real you. Why are you so afraid to let the real you out? The world is waiting. Stop neglecting the world, and more importantly, stop neglecting yourself!

Oh, but you think you can blame others for how your life is going? Really? Are you sure that something else or someone else is to blame for where you are in your life? That it's none of your doing? Maybe that's the problem. Maybe it's your lack of doing. Maybe it's because you let events and things that others do impact you in a way other than what you really want. Or maybe you just use it as an excuse. It's an excuse so you don't have to blame you for all the things you don't like about your life or even more common, what you don't like about yourself.

Is this really what you want? Does this really make you happy? Do you realize that you hold your peace and happiness entirely within you, where no one else can touch it? Do you realize that all it takes is a little effort to make your life blissful? I don't think many of us get this, or there'd be a heck of a lot more happy people walking around. Each and every one of us controls our happiness, our destiny, and who we are. No one else can control this for you, nor can you control it for anyone else. You can assist others, but you can never give them true peace. Each of us must accomplish this on our own, no matter what someone else is doing to us or for us.

So stop wallowing in your excuses and wake up! It's your fault, if you don't read on and realize it's all up to you. Instead of blasting it all to you at once, I'm gonna break this very important topic into parts and will do my best to not lecture too long on each. You can pursue each of these areas in much more depth through the sea of materials provided by tons of experts out there in other books, and it's pretty interesting stuff. I highly recommend you spend more time reading what the experts have written. What can it hurt? Here though, is what I'll be touching on:

1. You decide how something affects you, and how it continues to affect you. Even negative situations provide an opportunity for learning more about everything and everyone involved, including learning about yourself.
2. Each of us has free will and chooses exactly how we want our life to be, based on the amount of focus we give to everything. Clear thinking is the key to being in control of your life. When

you don't know exactly what you want, focus on asking for the best outcome.
3. Only you can make your choices. Listen to your deepest, truest feelings to know what choices to make. Always choose out of love for yourself and others, not out of fear of something.

Most of us acknowledge that no matter what life brings, we all have the power to decide how we're going to let it affect us. We decide what we take away from things that happen to us or around us. We know that we always have the choice to take away something positive and good, or something negative and bad. We can choose to learn from it or to harbor resentment over it.

So there you are, having a wonderful, productive day. Everything's flowing along and you feel great. Then, something completely illogical happens and suddenly, a crazed person is screaming at you at length, no matter how much you try to subdue them. They are completely irrational and you soon realize your yelling back is only sucking the energy and self-respect right out of you, and any eavesdroppers. Moreover, they're probably yelling at you for something that you had nothing to do with, but again, you can't get them to stop, no matter how you try to explain. You have two choices: Get violent and try to overpower them and physically shut them up (and probably get arrested over it, or worse), or realize you need to surrender and let them finish their psycho fit, no matter where that leaves you. The reasonable person has to choose defeat.

Suddenly, you are physically, mentally, and emotionally drained, all at the same time. You have nothing left for anything else. Your day is ruined. You either want to bark at the very next person you see, or crawl in a dark hole and nap until it all goes away. It sucks. This person just ruined your entire day, and then some. It might carry over past today and it might spill over onto other people, especially anyone that interacts with you.

If this frustrates you as much as it does me, please realize immediately, that it doesn't have to ruin your day. It really doesn't. How you let it affect you is still in your control. Acknowledge this, acknowledge the negative incident, decide why it bothered you and what you can do to make it stop bothering you, immediately! I know my pet peeves. My time was wasted. I was terribly disrespected. My neck and head ache now and I have no energy left to finish the rest of what I wanted to accomplish today. Moreover, I'll have to deal with the crazy person again, and I'm not looking forward to it! The "why" is acknowledged by thinking this through, along with the fact that the incident is over.

So next, I move on to what I can do to make it stop bothering me. Obviously, this person has issues and I did not deserve any of it, but I handled myself well by not loosing my temper. My patience was tested and I did not falter, at least, in front of them. I could care less if someone of that caliber respects me or not; I know they are not capable, as they do not respect themselves, as confirmed by their behavior. I am very grateful I am not that person, and I know it is my choice now, what I do with the rest of my day. Proud of my good behavior, I decide to reward myself a little, by taking a little time for me or with someone I'd enjoy spending time with. All of that only took a few minutes and ta-da! The negative impact from the situation is defeated! Moreover, I pressed myself to do something positive and actually ended up enhancing my day, all at the same time.

No matter what happens, you make continuous choices as to how it will influence you. Sometimes things happen to make us aware of our capabilities and our strengths, which supplies the additional courage we need to go after something bigger in our life. It happens to me all the time, so I do my best to remember, accept, and embrace whatever life brings. It brings a sense of peace along with it. No matter what's going on, it's all about what you make of it and how you let it affect you. It is your choice how it impacts you. While this is very true and so very important to remember, I'm going to go much deeper than that now, with how your prominent thoughts create your life, so please, continue on.

The entire world was created to accommodate human beings. When you think about something often or with a firm belief, you are actually summoning it to you. Now you may say that's too easy and there's no way it works, but I'll tell you from experience, it's not that easy to keep your head completely clear of things you DON'T want and completely believe in what you do want. But the more you practice it, the easier it becomes, and the faster you get what you wanted.

I can also tell you from experience, it does work. Be honest with yourself and take the time to think about the big things in your past. Think about both the good things and the bad things. Now, honestly, think through the connection to your thoughts before those things happened. Were they occupying your mind somewhere, possibly, in some shape or form? Whether it came from your upbringing, worrying, listening to people around you talk about it, hearing it on the news, or reading about it, it doesn't matter. Did it cross your mind? Do you see some connections?

I'm only passing along what I know. You should always believe in whatever you feel is right and beneficial to you and those around you, but this is one of those things. If it could help you have a better life, isn't it worth believing this? Don't you deserve that chance? Kind of like choosing to believe in God and heaven. One can choose not to believe, but as for me, I know God makes my life complete and I've got nothing to lose and so much to gain, believing. Every once in a while, I hear the silly challenge, "There's no proof God exists." Well, I know He does, so I don't waste my time arguing and pointing out how so many people have given account after account that He does. But I can't help but wonder how they can't feel silly saying this, because sooner or later, someone's going to challenge them and ask, "What proof do you have that He DOESN'T exist?"

Getting back to the topic, as I mentioned earlier, God's gift of free will allows us to define who we want to be and what we want our life to be. Our life follows our thoughts—our most prominent and dominant thoughts. The ones that deep, deep down, we truly believe. It doesn't matter if the thoughts are good or bad, positive or negative. Words like don't are ignored; free will only acknowledges the main topic. So even if you say, "I don't want to get sick," your free will is thinking about sickness. Think about health instead, as in "I'm always healthy, no matter what's going on around me." Whatever you focus on—and I mean whole-heartedly, without a doubt, focus on—you get. You get the main subject of what you think, regardless of whether it's positive or negative, so pay attention to what you're thinking about!

Second, if you think things like "I need" or "I want" it creates needing or wanting and holds you in the status of needing or wanting. It makes it a future, unobtainable item that you are wanting or needing. Remove those words and use "I am thankful I have" or "I am thankful I will have it now or I will have it soon." Anything to remove the wanting or needing and put it in the present. Does that make sense?

Let me give you some examples:

If you think...	*...you get...*
I am too busy	too busy
I have lots of time	lots of time
I always lose	loss
I'm very lucky	luck
I have too much debt	debt
I have to save money	the need to save money
I have lots of money	extra money
I have to lose weight	the need to lose weight
The weight is coming off	less weight
I'm going to catch that virus	sick
I won't get sick	sick
I'm always healthy	health
I don't want to be late	late

Take a few minutes now and write down a few of your beliefs, thoughts, and worries. Make a quick list of anything and everything you really believe, deep down, about yourself or about your life. Now make the second column and pick out the MAIN IDEA of each thought, including the words want or need, or the like. They're not all so positive, are they? Do they coincide with what your past experiences have been or where you are presently, in your life? If you're being completely honest in this exercise, I know many of them do relate back directly to something in your life, so really take a little time to realize all of this. Crazy, isn't it? But now that you understand this, it's crazy good!

Look at your list some more and focus on anywhere you wrote words like have to, need, or want. Realize these words will keep you in the state of needing or wanting these things, never in the state of having it. Now I know your desire is really to have it, not to constantly need it, so let's work on changing those thoughts first. You need positive wording to replace the record you've been planning over and over again, in your mind. It might be easiest to start with the opposite of it, or maybe focus on the end result, instead. Here are some examples from my previous list:

Instead of thinking…	*…think this…*
I have to save money	My savings account is growing
I have to lose weight	I am slimming down more every day

I don't care if you believe the phrase at the moment, just start out by re-phrasing your beliefs to be what you truly want for yourself. Next, continue on with the other items on your list that are negative in any way and replace them with something positive, again, ignoring whether you believe it right now or not.

Here are more examples from my previous list:

Instead of thinking...	*...think this...*
I am too busy	I have plenty of time to do the things I want
I don't want to be late	I am always a few minutes early

Once you've created new phrases to replace the unwanted ones, you can start changing these things immediately. First off, though, you have to really want to change it, or you'll keep yourself from believing, which will keep it from you. You may need to practice and work your way up to truly believing your new phrases, and that's just fine. Often though, just realizing that you've been holding yourself back launches a great amount of determination, and it's not unheard of to change something you've been struggling with overnight. The amount of time it takes depends on the effort, focus, and belief you put into it, and once you master one thought, you'll be anxious to work on the others. Trust me!

Greater focus comes easily when you add appreciation for the desired item, so I highly recommend it. For instance, you could say, "I'm so relieved I will be a few minutes early," or "I feel great and appreciate my healthier body and the high amount of energy I have now." Gratitude will drastically reduce the amount of time it takes to retrain your thoughts and to obtain the end result you truly want. Use it often!

Once again, you have to believe the renewed thought whole-heartedly. If you want to change your luck or gain time, your mind must first completely believe it. Have faith and know you deserve it and your life will follow. I needed, and still need, plenty of training on focusing to achieve this. I know I can pursue this desire by first thinking, "I am grateful I am aware of my thoughts and know I have everything I think clearly about. I am mastering this process more and more, everyday." One tool I use often to stay focused is <u>The Secret</u>, by Rhonda Byrne. I listen to this book on CD often when I'm driving, over and over, until I feel like I'm focused on that particular aspect of my life. It's been very helpful to me in giving me basics and ideas to retrain my thinking to get what I want in my life. Another of my favorites, <u>Conversations with God</u>, by Neale Donald Walsch, deepened my perspective and helped me to accept that using free will to control my life works together with God's intentions for our purpose in life. Knowing this helps me to sharpen my thoughts on what I want, and the easier it becomes. I'm giving it attention. I'm giving it more prominent thoughts, and this brings all of it to me, as God designed.

So if our thoughts lead our life, what happens when you're not clear and focused on what you want? Well, your life will naturally follow, and so, it doesn't know where to go. Events in your day will be random, possibly even chaotic at times, because you haven't given any instructions as to how it should be. Your day will be as murky as your thoughts. Worse, anything you are worrying about or thinking about, deep down, is being encouraged to happen because it's probably your dominant thought! *You may also ask, what if I don't know what I want?* What if I'm not sure how I want things to go or what I want to do? Again, this is a very normal occurrence throughout our life. Simple. Ask and believe that the best outcome for you and others will happen. Think about all the good outcomes and know that whatever happens, you will embrace it and know it is what's best, even if it's hard to understand at the time. Remind yourself that God knows what He's doing and ask Him to do what is best for you. Very often, it will become clear, later on down the line. Be patient and have faith when the answers don't come as quickly or as clearly as you'd like. Keep an open mind and very likely, you will understand why things had to be a certain way. Just realize, it may take a while to see it.

Skeptical? I'm betting you are. We certainly don't want to be the one to blame for things we complain about. But do you want to make your life better? Well then, it's up to you. Try this theory out for a week, even on one simple thought, with an open and accepting mind, and just see what happens. Focus on your new phrase every chance you get, and truly believe it and appreciate it, and feel like you'd feel having it. What have you got to lose? Another week of coasting through the chaos, that's what.

Here are some basics that really help me:

1. Fall asleep and wake up, knowing how you want your day to go. See yourself vividly in the events and really think about how you'd feel as things go perfectly. Allow yourself to be happy and content, knowing everything will flow perfectly.
2. Ask God for, and be thankful for, this perfect day and all you've been blessed with.
3. Think positive thoughts only, all day long! Avoid or release any negativity, worry, or use of "I don't want" or "I don't have" immediately! You must be convinced and focused on what is in your perfect

day and events! The way you word your thoughts is everything. If nothing else, think, "I am grateful for this smooth, organized, relaxing day and everything I am accomplishing today." Be specific and see yourself getting through each task or event perfectly and know how great you will feel as it happens.
4. Have faith and completely believe. God tells us to have faith in what He's created for us. His gift of free will brings us whatever we truly focus on. But if we don't make the effort to focus on it and believe, deep down, He cannot bring it to us. He leaves it up to us to decide.
5. As you get what you envisioned, take a moment to thank God and give back often by being kind to others.
6. Distance yourself from, or ignore negative people, comments, or news, realizing this distracts you and makes YOU think negatively when you are exposed to it. Push out any such thoughts quickly by thinking, "I'm so grateful I am who I am," or get specific about what you possess that this person or news event does not have, for instance, "I appreciate my safe neighborhood." Trust me, avoiding the newspapers, TV, and radio news does wonders here!
7. Repeat this process every single day and realize that any bad days you have were allowed in by your not focusing on these very basic things. If bad days happen, it's okay to accept that we are only human and that growth is a main part of our life, and then re-focus as soon as possible.

While your primary focus (your free will) drives most everything that comes into your life, your choices drive what you do with it, obviously. Every choice you make, big or small, can affect your life and have an impact on the world. The choices you make determine whether you get the life that you want. If you make choices to push away your dreams or to prevent them from becoming reality, obviously, they can't come to be. I am continuously baffled by people that make choices to keep what they say they want from happening. It's almost like they think they don't deserve it or really just don't want it, so they actually prevent it from happening. It's a scary mind they live with, I think, and such a shame, especially if they complain that they'll "never have their dreams!" Ugh! I just want to wake them up and tell them to kick their own ass! Do they know how ridiculous they are? Do they realize how much of their life they are wasting? Do they know what a burden they are on others who have faith in them? It's very frustrating to me.

Now I'm not perfect, so I don't always make choices to get what I want, either. But I do try to realize it and dig down into my brain to figure out why I did what I did. Once I know why, I can choose to do something about it, and try not to make the same mistake again. Thank goodness I have people around me that care and bother to point out when I'm about to make a choice that I won't be happy with later! We need each other for this! None of us is perfect or thinks clearly, all the time.

So choices are there in front of us, all day long. Choices on how you'll start your day. Choices on what you do with your day. Choices on how you behave and what you believe. Decisions. Compromises. Advice. Opportunities, both subtle and obvious ones. Choices, choices, choices! Make sure they are supporting your dreams and who you want to be and not fighting against them. This includes the choice to "stay neutral." A neutral stance really means you're choosing not to do something or believe something, which is the same as not choosing it, and thus, choosing the opposite. In a lot of things, there really is no true "neutral." Your lack of action displays your choice, or at least, gives others an impression of which way you are leaning, which can be just as powerful as choosing it outright. Take a common question, like "Do you believe in God?" If someone says, "Yes," or "No," you know where they stand. If someone doesn't reply or says, "I don't know," you take that more as a "No" than anything, right? So lack of support for the "Yes" tells you they support the "No." Keep this in mind next time you're being wishy-washy or deciding not to get involved. Realize you are making your opinion clear, even through lack of action. Make sure it's the impression you wanted to give.

If you're having a hard time choosing, break it down into two sides to make it simple. There's the fear side and there's the love side. So first off, ask yourself, am I leaning towards this choice because of something I'm afraid of, like the worst result that could happen, what people will think of me, or what someone has said about it? Is it a fear that is driving my decision? Then think more clearly and ask yourself honestly, what would really make me feel good? What would genuine, fearless love do? Whether it's love and fulfillment for yourself or caring for others, it's all the same. If you boil it down to this simplest level, you can't go wrong. Choosing or deciding something with love is always the "right" choice, no matter what happens after. You will know you did the best you could and didn't allow fear or lies to talk you into making a choice you didn't feel good about. Love always brings good. Fear will always leave you feeling defeated, regretful, and incomplete. It's easy enough; all you have to do is think it through and the choice or direction will be very clear to you.

Practice choosing with love and it will become a habit you will be very satisfied with.

Moreover, if you have a thought, but don't support it with your actions and choices, maybe you're not really aware of your deepest, truest thought. Take an example of thinking you want to be healthy, but then make a choice of lighting up a cigarette. The action contradicts the thought completely, so maybe you need to look at your real, deep-down thought again? Maybe you really don't want to be completely healthy? Maybe you think you need to be unhealthy, or don't deserve health? Yes, it sounds insane; I guess it kind of is, when you really don't know what your innermost thoughts really are. Take some time and get to the bottom of it, being completely honest with yourself, so that you can change those embedded apprehensions. Other sections of this book should get you started, but again, there's a wealth of assistance out there, everywhere you turn. Someone's struggled with it and conquered it before, believe me!

One last thing we all need to keep in mind, as we watch others sabotage themselves, through their thoughts and actions. You can offer your advice, opinions, or assistance to help someone else, and if they ask, you usually should. Just remember that they must choose for themselves. Each person can only control their own life, through everything I've touched on in this section; no one else has any power over you, and you have no power over anyone else. Individuals must make their own decisions and control their own actions. Even when it's apparent to you someone is making a mistake or enabling a bad situation, it's not entirely up to you. It's up to them. Even when someone cries on your shoulder and swears they want to change something, only their actions can confirm their commitment. Deep down, they may not really be ready to change, or perhaps, they really don't ever want to change. Do your best to be patient with them and if they ask, to help them to discover why they continue to make the choices they do. You'll know when it's time to shelter yourself from any negativity they bring, as it's possible they enjoy the drama and attention. Be honest with them and let them know you can't believe they want things to be different until you see them making some progress and changes. Be there to give them a pat on the back when they do. Be there to share this insight with them, as you never know when they might be listening and be open to it.

The control you have over your own life is powerful, isn't it? It's amazing to me. Promise yourself to re-read this chapter and practice all of these very important things over and over until this is the way you live. Then, come back to this chapter about once a month and do your lists again to see your progress and what you still need to work on. Don't give up. Ever! God created us with abilities beyond our wildest imaginations. Allow yourself to learn and expand your thinking beyond what you always thought free will was. We know God wants us to live in a state of heaven, so doesn't it make sense? He lets us choose everything about our lives and everything about who we want to be. He made His decisions with love and gave us all the ability to decide what our bliss will be. He lets us decide what our heaven will be! He is there to help us, constantly, but He gave us complete responsibility for ourselves. He gave us the incredible gift of free will, a means to have anything we want.

ARE YOU TELLING PEOPLE YOU'RE NOT WORTH A SH**?

 **People can't like you, if you don't like you.**

You've heard the saying, "People can't like you until you like you first." It's true, you know. It's nearly impossible for someone to REALLY like you and want to get close to you, if you don't like you first. If you don't like yourself, you are warning everyone else to stay away. You're telling them you're not a positive person to know. Here are some outward, obvious signs that you don't think you're the best person you can be:

- Lying, which includes not telling the whole truth and giving answers you don't know are right. You do this to try to appear you know everything because you're insecure. You mislead people with your response, which could possibly lead to harm. Soon, they realize you are a liar and will steer clear of you. If you don't know the answer, it's better to begin your response with, "I'm not sure, but…"

- Having a negative attitude; you usually think about the bad things that could happen or did happen instead of looking for the good in things. You also dwell on the negative things about people and sometimes even point them out to others in a sad attempt to make yourself look better. It doesn't work, though. You only end up making yourself look bad.

- Being a "taker." The world flows when people give and take. When someone takes more than they give, it throws everything off. If you only give to get something you want, and rarely because you really want to help someone, you're a taker.

- Not taking care of yourself (physically, mentally, and emotionally). It's a no-brainer. If you like yourself, you make a strong attempt at taking care of your health, your mental state (stress), and your emotional state (keeping a clear head when it comes to relationships). You take care of yourself because you find value in taking care of yourself. You realize that being healthy puts you in a good position to fulfill your desires in life and in a good state to help others, instead of being a burden to them.

Most people are drawn to people who like themselves and do not appear to have any of the above "diseases." People like real. People like positive energy. People usually do not want people with a coating of SH** on them. Again, they'd rather stay clear and not catch the disease. Moreover, if you have this disease, you're probably not a whole bunch of fun to be around! People like real, upbeat, fun people and they hope some of THAT rubs off on them.

If I described you above, don't despair. I need to remind you of something very important. You are in control of you. You can change your behavior at any second. Just because you might have done one of these things a minute ago doesn't mean you have to continue doing it! Remember, you are the boss of you!

Face it though. You might be negative for a reason. You might not be able to talk yourself into taking care of yourself that easily. It's totally understandable. Please, please, please repeat the following to yourself constantly, if you need to, to start working on changing your mind:

- "Whatever happened in the past, is in the past." Unless you can do something huge to make up for it, leave it in the past and look forward! You do not have to drag it along today.

- "I am a human being, and I deserve a good place on the earth, just as much as the next guy." If you don't feel like you've done anything to earn that place, well, get started today then. Right now!

- "I will do small acts of kindness for people." Do this for people you know and for complete strangers. Then, be prepared to see how good it makes you feel. Most of the time, the good feeling you get is bigger than how you made the other person feel. You can't lose! And when you can, do BIG acts of kindness, too.

- "I will be honest with myself about what is bringing me down, holding me back, and what I'd like to do differently, both with how I approach life and how I take care of myself. I can't be all I'm supposed to be if I don't take care of myself. I promise myself I will take at least one step every day towards changing this." It can be a baby step, or a huge leap if you're really fed up with things—whatever trips your trigger. Again, you decide. You take care of you!

Remember, if you don't like yourself enough to be your own best friend, why would anyone else want to be your best friend? Instead of being your own worst enemy, realize you are important to this world, and you're here for a good reason. Start taking care of yourself and start behaving in a positive way, and then watch people come to you!

DON'T SIT AND SPIN IN THE SH**!

Sometimes you are supposed to walk away and not go back.

Seriously, do yourself a favor and move forward! Especially with relationships that don't work out. Why spend all your time rehashing the illogical things that were said and done in trying to make the other person understand your point of view? Why try over and over to reason with them? Just accept that they don't want to be reasonable and they don't give a SH** about your point of view. You are being given strong validation that this relationship is NOT meant to be, so why are you being so stupid and banging your head against the wall? Is all that negativity good for anybody? Time for you to go!

I'm not saying that as soon as one or two little things go wrong, you should bail. Not at all! In fact, I think that it's a shame that people are so lazy and insecure when they walk away from something, just because someone doesn't share their same opinion on something, especially when it has NO DIRECT IMPACT on what happens in their life. Say for instance, over a political stance, when you're not employed by the government.

You are entitled to your opinion and thoughts on everything, but if it doesn't have any bearing on your day-to-day relationship with someone that doesn't agree with you, who cares! You want them to have a brain and their own thoughts, don't you? We would all be very boring clones, if we all had the same viewpoints. So let these things go! This applies to other things too, like the way someone cleans the house or gets ready to go out. Maybe it's not exactly how you would do it, but as long as it's getting accomplished, does it really matter how it's getting done? Don't be such a low-life to monster-size these stupid little things into negative feelings in your relationship!

So what I'm talking about are major, getting-no-where BIG problems in relationships. Something that you've asked the other person not to do, over and over again, because there is harm or damage, or high risk to someone or something because of it. Maybe they're being disrespectful to you or someone else in your household. Maybe they create problems constantly, adding major drama to your life or someone else's life. Maybe they're taking advantage of you and just using you, your money, your possessions, etc. Maybe they lie to you and create a constant negative environment in your household. By all means, talk to them calmly and thoroughly, and do all you can to help them understand how it affects you or others in your life. Do everything you can imagine to try to help them understand and to try to help improve the situation safely, and within reason. But once you've exhausted all options including getting outside help, and that person is still not showing sincere progress, you need to accept that maybe they do not want to change things. You need to accept that you are not meant to be with that person. Don't take it personally, don't resent, don't morn. Just do what's best for all of you and close the relationship, being honest, direct, and calm with the other person, and then walk away!

And when I say walk away, I mean walk away! Do not carry the baggage, the resentment, the confusion, or the second-guessing along with you! URG! That is the worst! Resentment is ugly, no matter who is looking at you, and no matter how much you try to justify your bitterness. No matter what, people don't like crabby, bitter, or negative anything. They don't want to get any of your crap on them! Get over it first and then go socialize. When it comes to second-guessing yourself, stop and think before you allow it to happen! You had probably threatened calling it quits with this person before, but obviously, you never followed through completely. They know this, and they probably think this is just another idle threat. They probably know you well enough to tell if you really mean what you say or not, so make sure you are absolutely going to do what's best for you, this time.

Remember, you must take care of your own emotions and needs before you can really be there for anyone else. Remind yourself over and over, why the relationship has to end. Don't fool yourself with the limited memories of the "good times" when the bad times far outweigh them. When you start second-guessing yourself by fading back to the good time, pull yourself back to the facts of the bad things. Do you treat people you care about that way? Of course not! So you have to stick to the fact that the person mistreating you either doesn't care or can't care enough to stop. That's the fact, and that's what you need to be focusing on. Healthy relationships are almost completely "good times." When people are compatible, they just get along. Those kind of relationships do exist and are readily available when you're with the right person. Allow yourself to move on to the things you've always wanted, so that you realize how your life should be and how good it feels! Sleep on it, don't look back, and don't falter. You only take massive steps backwards when you react when you're weak with emotions. Do not communicate with that person whatsoever until you are positively sure of what you need to do for yourself!

Now, once you've done what's best for you, you automatically do what's best for others, including the very person you said goodbye to. After all, as you allow the undesirable situations to go on, you enable and encourage the bad behavior to continue. It not only harmed you, but it harmed them as well, because there was no reason for them to alter what they were doing. Some people need brutal honesty to make them realize what they are doing, and perhaps make them reconsider it in the future. They need someone to stop their pattern of recklessness or irresponsibility. It helps them understand that it is not an acceptable way to behave. Moreover, if there was anyone else affected by your relationship, you have helped them, too. This includes people you interact with at any time, including the future, as you will be more content, and more open and giving. You can show your true colors and pursue what you really want to. You can give the world the real you. So remember this always: You automatically help everyone around you when you do what is best for you. You can't go wrong making the right choice and it will get your life out of the SH** hole and back on track!

NEED TO SHOW EVERYBODY YOU'RE AN IMPORTANT SH**?

Rudeness tells people how little you really think of yourself.

Think you're telling the world you're important with rude, demanding behavior? Well, let me give you a big fat dose of reality. People think of words that start with the letter "i" alright. Your behavior sends a broadcast to the world that you're an impatient, intolerant, insecure, insignificant idiot! The word "important" does not cross their minds at all, trust me! They may think of words that start with the letter "a" too, like arrogant, attention seeking, and the other word for donkey. People know you go through your day looking for ways to speak or behave in a rude way to make someone stop and notice you.

They notice, alright. They notice you are so unhappy with your life and so disappointed in who you are that you have no self-discipline whatsoever, and that you are too weak to focus with any other little distraction in your immediate environment. Take background noise of other people, for instance. It's classic, especially if there's children involved. Are you one of these pathetic people that have to complain about reasonable sounds coming from other people in public places, like buses or bus stops, airplanes or airports, restaurants, churches, or libraries? Or worse yet, are you rude about it or blame your inability to focus on it? Wow. That's sad.

Well, maybe you should live in a sound-proof bubble or better yet, a remote cave, far from civilization. Invest in those noise-blocking headphones and wear them everywhere you go! Oh, but you might still be able to see those people, having more fun than you are and you might notice they enjoy life. So, you'd better throw on a blindfold too, while you're at it. There. Now you can't see or hear anyone that might annoy you. You can avoid all that stress, altogether! Do yourself a favor and ask for blindness and deafness in your next life; I'm sure you'll be happier that way.

Another all-too-predictable behavior of you unwise people, is the rudeness you show to people in the service industries. You think that you have more money, education, or a better job, and therefore, need to remind people "below" you of this. Sadly enough, it only displays your lack of intelligence, lack of professionalism, and lack of happiness, and not a one of these people would ever envy you. They are more than aware of your sick behavior with the desire to bring down another, and would never want to imitate you. In fact, they often use you as an example when teaching their children how not to be behave! You really don't want to know what they really think of you. I am amazed at you people every time I visit a restaurant, fly on a plane, or watch any blue collar worker come to the rescue to build or fix something for some clueless "professional." There is nothing professional about an idiot that is rude to the very people that do a job to provide convenience, comfort, or any luxuries that you'd be too helpless to manage without them. Then where would your grand life be? Be nice to people, especially when they are just trying to be nice to you and trying to help you, because they realize your intellectual, emotional, and social limitations. They don't even mind that you're truly on a level far beneath them!

DEMAND RESPECT? YOU'VE LOST IT!

You cause a tremendous amount of harm when you're a jerk, mostly to yourself.

Demand respect? Really? Did you think about that one? You know better. We know better. There are certain things that cannot be taken from someone. They have to be given freely. Things like love, loyalty, honesty, compassion, and gee, guess what else? Respect. If that's what you're looking for, you are going about it all wrong, being a jerk. And guess what? You are having the opposite affect on your poor recipient. They are NOT respecting you, no matter what they say or do for you. Out of necessity and their self-dignity, they may tolerate you, but they certainly don't respect you.

They may think that you're a miserable, crazy person in need of therapy. They may do their best to keep the waters calm, but they absolutely will not respect you. No one likes or looks up to someone that doesn't have enough self-pride to treat others decent. When you do not treat others kindly, you broadcast to the world you are a miserable being with low self-worth. We've all heard the saying, you need to treat others with respect to earn it, and it's absolutely true. To respect someone means to admire, honor, approve, and revere them. How can someone have these feelings about you if you don't give them any reason to even like you?

So wow, when you start feeling crabby and are on the verge of taking it out on anyone that comes in contact with you, think twice and realize you are exposing your naked weakness and inflicting an extreme amount of harm to both yourself and to others. It's time for someone to knock you aside the head and wake you up! It might as well be me. I'll lay the basics down for you first, and then prove it to you with an everyday example. I dare you to read on for a couple of your important minutes.

My base is the fact that everyone's connected, and as you hurt others, you hurt yourself even more. Many different spiritual teachings will tell you the same thing, no matter what origin or part of the world the teaching comes from. Most point to everything being ONE. One being, one universe, or at least that everything is connected to everything else. Now you can choose to ignore all thoughts and feeling on the topic, and say, "I don't believe in all that crap!" But the fact remains, somehow, all of these different beliefs and teachings of these beliefs somehow have something in common. I find that very interesting, and you should too. While you may not realize the direct, immediate impact to you, trust me, in the end, it does harm you. So my point is, do you really dislike yourself that much that you would purposely impose misery or hardship on yourself? Think about it and read on to my everyday example.

Maybe one morning, you wake up grumpy. You aren't overly bubbly or nice to anyone in your household, in fact, you criticize and complain about little, pointless things. You eventually drag yourself to your car and into work, and continue with the same unappealing attitude when you encounter people through your job. Typical, right? Well, now think through the likely impact to people and situations around you.

Your wife thinks you're miserable in your marriage and unhappy with your life. She has pretty much given up trying to help you to be happy, and just stays out of your way. She refrains from showing you too much affection because you diss her when you're in this kind of mood. You are not as appealing to her anymore and it probably shows in your intimacy life, if you still have much of one. She may stay loyal to you, but dreams of the man she fell in love with, either returning to her some day, or moving on so she can be with someone more caring some day. Your moodiness stresses her out and burdens her as she moves through her day. Your mood may keep her from being the fun, creative, successful person she was meant to be.

Your kids may try to ignore you, but they can't help but always care about their parents and whether or not they are happy. Unfortunately, this is a burden most children carry around with them, their whole life, regardless of whether the parent deserves this kind of concern from anyone else. They too, have probably given up trying to make you happy and just try to stay out of your way. It's only natural for them to start to care less and less about you, because it causes them too much distress when you aren't doing anything to make yourself happy. They may even start to think that it's partially their fault, which takes a major hit on the self-esteem of a growing person, and will hold them back from pursuing simple things as well as their life dreams. It could take years for them to move beyond the damage, or they may not at all, adding one more miserable, stifled adult to the world some day.

Lovely so far, huh? You may think I'm exaggerating, but maybe sometime when your family isn't feeling threatened by your mood, you should very gently ask them what they think when you're in that kind of a mood. They may care about you too much to answer honestly, but you should be able to see by the look in their eyes, a little of how they really feel.

Then there's anyone else you come in contact with, all day; I could keep going and going. The people you work with think you have some serious mental and emotional issues. They may do what they have to, to keep their job, but secretly hope that working with you will be temporary, as they do not like you. They probably talk about you constantly, behind your back, so that everyone else is painfully aware of your defects as well. They hope in the phrase, "What comes around, goes around."

Is anything sinking in? I hope so, for your sake. It is never too late to start damage control. Just promise to like yourself and others enough for just a little while and read a few more sections of this book. Even a little peace is better than where you're at, right?

Having people respect you is easy, so pay attention! Respect comes when people know you're being straight with them. Respect is really just a form of admiration. Think about it. Who do you respect? Why? It's the same way when people look at you.

Don't pull no SH**! Be honest with people and be

reliable for them. Show them this respect and it will be returned, at least the majority of the time. Offer your help when you can, especially to people that really deserve it or when they really need it. It won't go unnoticed. People remember. People observe.

Also, remember that only you control your behavior. If the crowd is moving towards something that's not exactly what you want, that you don't need to go along with it. NEVER flow with SH**. Make your own choices. You'll never regret it, and again, people will respect you for it.

One more thing. Don't give people SH**. Try your best to influence people in a positive way; steer clear of causing any negative vibes. Negativity from you won't make you proud of yourself and it gives others a reason to not like you. Moreover, think about what goes hand-in-hand with your feelings towards someone you don't like. You don't respect them either, do you?

If you want to change your behavior to earn people's respect, remember, you can begin immediately! You are in control of your actions!   As you're learning to be a more upright person, it helps sometimes to imitate someone that you think is "The SH**." Think about how they act, what they say, and how they would react to certain situations.

Think about it. When people are talking about you, would it be so bad if they say, "Yeah, he/she is a good SH**!"

DON'T ADD TO THE SH** PILE!

 **Negative comments hurt others, but hurt the speaker more.**

I have a theory as to why some people seem to continually add to the SH** pile. I think the main reason people are negative is because they have some sick idea that if they make another pile bigger, no one will notice the humongous pile they're dragging around with them.

If you ever do this, are you for real? Again, I challenge that you've never really thought through this, have you? Don't you realize that when you're negative, you are broadcasting to the world that you have a huge pile of SH** on you? You're not hiding anything. People try to stand back from people like you because even though they don't know what's in your pile or how big it is, they don't want to get any on their shoes. They know it's there!

The most annoying pile-builders are the complainers …the whiners. The kind that are just constantly bitching about something, but never, ever have a solution. The crap they add really stinks. They add negativity and stress to anyone close, within earshot, as well as to anyone very far away, that may feel it from the domino effect. The domino effect occurs when someone within earshot isn't as positive to the next person as they should be, because of the negativity that was just smeared on them. This domino effect can go on forever, I think. The only thing stopping it is someone with enough awareness and intelligence to not pass it along.

Sometimes complaints are valid and necessary, but tell me, what good do they do if the complainer isn't offering a solution? Furthermore, what good is it if the complainer isn't willing to assist with the solution? So many weak people complain all day long, but they'll never step an inch towards trying to fix it. It's just random SH**, and seriously, they have a personal problem of some sort if they are constantly wasting their breath on this type of thing.

A lot of the time, people are open to solutions and to the assistance of someone that cares to change things for the better. When presented in a positive way, people will often be very receptive to new ideas. The pile-builders, however, are not really interested in making things better. They feast on something to complain about, and again, are terribly disillusioned because they think it hides their pile, which just grows with every pointless complaint. Besides, if the problem was resolved, they'd just move on to something else to complain about. They are their own worst enemy.

Close behind the top offender are the judgmental people with all the negative opinions. Again, unless you're proposing a solution and are committed to following it through, you're just adding to the heap and putting your own heap on display.

Worst of all, when you pile crap on top of someone else, you're putting an equal share (or possibly more) on your pile at the same time. It makes other people feel bad, but it lowers your respect for yourself even more; naturally, you will not feel great about yourself. Your conscience or destiny will catch up to you eventually.

So don't add to the SH** pile. There are so many other good things you could be doing. The first step is to just keep your mouth shut, for if no crap is emitted out of the pie hole, none is added. The second step is to move up a notch and offer to help with solutions and more important, to follow through. This cuts down some of the height of the pile. And finally, if you're a strong enough person, you'll very kindly make other people aware of their negative actions, when they're adding to the pile, and let them know you don't care to hear it. Even if you have a good effect every once in a while, you make a good chunk of that pile disappear. Somebody's gotta do it, or we'd all be buried in the stuff!

IF YOU CAN'T SAY SOMETHING NICE…

 **Kind words have much more power than mean words and they don't expose your ugliness.**

Seriously, if you can't say something nice, you should probably keep the pie hole closed! Gossip gets so out-of-control, so easily, and 99% of the time, it's just feeding into the almighty river we've been talking about. Please take a minute to think about this!

Communication, written, verbal, or visual is such a powerful thing! A nice gesture or compliment to someone that's having an awful day can turn their day around, and renew their faith in people. So often, a nice thought comes to our mind. You wonder how someone you know is doing. You see an acquaintance with a new hairstyle that looks great on them. You watch a nervous child struggling to please someone. Nice thoughts, let out through the pie hole, can make a real difference to people.

Call or email that person you're thinking about. Tell the acquaintance you really like their hair. Encourage the child with some kind words. Never let an opportunity to help someone with such little effort pass by. I don't care how small it is; anytime you have a nice thought, don't trap it in a useless place. I for one, appreciate it when people do this for me. Had it not been for a few people telling me, "You should really write!" I may never have been bold enough to change my career at 40-something years old!

Kind words help me to know I'm on the right track, when I'm not certain of myself. It gives me the courage to do more of it. Some of us, in our effort to maintain our modesty, forget to be proud of the good things we do and belittle our talents and the gifts we have to offer to the world. Most of this book's inspiration came from the wonderful friends and complete strangers that bothered to say a few kind words to me; it raised my self-esteem and confidence a tremendous amount. It was so simple. One instance I'll never forget came from a wonderful man that I barely knew. He asked me what I did, and I proceeded to tell him, starting with the words, "I just …" He patiently waited for me to finished, smiled warmly at me and said, "You shouldn't say it like that. You should be proud of that and say it with more confidence." Without offending me, he offered some kind help that he was not obligated to do, whatsoever. I was touched deeply by it and stopped to think about my words before they came out of my mouth, from that point forward. After I realized how much kind words and gestures supported me, I vowed to be conscious of the opportunities I had to do the same for others. Try it out. You'll see. And wait until you see how good it makes you feel!

In a perfect world, negative communications would not take place. But the reality is, all too quickly, harsh words flood the river, and soon it's out of control. Often, we speak, email, or send a text message in hurt and haste. We don't think about the image we send about ourselves. We don't think about the tremendous damage it could cause. We are weak. And later, if you're really honest with yourself, you admit to yourself that it made you feel icky. Even if the person really deserved it, it doesn't make us proud. It makes us feel like we stooped to their level, like we took a dip in the SH**. So what do you do?

Well, there's times when you have to say something to someone to let them know they can't get away with it, and there's times when you need to warn other people that may be harmed. That's an exception of when you should say something, but choose your words carefully if you don't want to be categorized on their level. Try to stick to the facts and leave out the swear words and anger. You'll be glad that you can walk away with your dignity.

Now the majority of the time, though, there's no real justification for negative communications like gossiping, teasing, and judging out loud. A good rule to follow is, will it bring good to the people hearing or reading it, or benefit the person you're talking about? If not, just save it. Text messaging and instant messaging is really out of hand these days. Close behind is emailing, chat, and in-person gossip. Stop and think before you start another stream of SH** that grows into a river when the people you said it to repeat it, and finally, into a deeper and deeper pit of SH**. Where else is it going to go?

The problem here, is you've started some ickiness now, and it just spreads from there. You may think it's harmless, but consider this for a moment. All the people you communicated with are being pulled into your crap by reading or hearing something negative. It is not helping them, it is harming them. Now they repeat it, which coats them in the stuff, and the people they told repeat it, etc. Now, you've negatively affected many, many people and absolutely have harmed whomever you were talking about, fair or unfair. You probably also hurt some of the innocent people around the person you're gossiping about. Does that really make you feel good? What if one of your nasty comments became one of the reasons that person leans towards suicide? What if that person was abused in the past and is really messed up? Do you really know what goes on in that person's life? How do you think you could possibly know all the facts? How do you know that everything others have said is completely true? Why do you feel the need to hurt them? Do you think that by pointing out other people's flaws you look better? Where did you get such a ridiculous idea? Hurting others ALWAYS makes you look like a loser. It's an obvious sign that you are insecure or unhappy. It looks bad on you, and it really is that simple.

So, the challenge is, instead of taking your jabs when you could to knock somebody that's down, don't judge, and demonstrate some self-control. I know I don't appreciate jealous lies that have been spoken about me throughout my life—especially to dear friends that actually believed them and severed our friendship. I supposed the friendship was meant to end, if they believed so easily, but shame on both the speaker and the listener! I feel bad that they were so weak and insecure, to not know better. Change your habits to forgo the negative conversations and focus on positive ones instead. When you have the least, little, something nice to say to or about someone, let it flow! Just rise above, my friend, rise above!

Communication, written or spoken, is such a powerful thing. Why not keep it beautiful? Why drag it through the SH**? Why allow your mouth or hands to spew SH**? Ewe! Regardless of what your misled mind thinks at the time, no one really enjoys getting sprinkled with the stuff! On the other hand, positive communication can help everyone that hears it, and everyone that passes it along. Truth be told, this is why I write. I hope my writing leaves a positive impression with you and helps you to avoid most of the SH** that might flow your way!

DID YOU GET LOST IN A RELATIONSHIP, SOMEWHERE?

Let the changes in, be your true self, and you will find yourself again.

As you enter into new relationships or changes in your life, what is your reaction? Are you a defensive player that does all to protect your "current self" or are you an offensive team player, open to altering your behavior for the good of the team? By team, I mean any others involved AS WELL AS yourself. Is it good for all of you? We all handle this differently, from one extreme to the other. The key is balance and flexibility. With these, not only will others be very content around you, but you will feel satisfaction and contentment as well.

So let's start on one end, with people that refuse to let anything or anyone "change" them. You'll hear them say, "I don't do anything just because someone tells me to!" Or, "Having a baby is NOT going to change my life!" Now you would think that someone with such strong statements has a perfectly happy life and thinks they are the perfect being. Well, too bad that's not true. Too bad, just the opposite is true. In fact, if you think about it, what they're really broadcasting to the rest of us is that they can barely handle life the way it is and they are terrified they can't handle giving anything to anyone else.

So sad. All they have to do is open one teenier-tiny section of their brain and think about what they're really feeling, deep down. They are not completely happy, or they wouldn't be so incredibly uncomfortable with the idea of change. Change is probably the only thing that can begin to bring them the life they want! Change allows all of us to explore things we didn't know about ourselves and others, which opens more opportunities for growth. Change is damn good!

The person afraid of change will grow miserable, as they cling to their old life and try to make the square pegs of their old activities and behaviors fit into the round holes of their new life. They may feel aggravated or defeated, and take it out on any and all innocent bystanders. Sadly, they don't move on with their significant other, and they begin to bicker and even resent each other, as they can't understand each other. The hardheaded non-changer has lost who they are and is also denying those around them what they deserve—their true self.

Then, we have people on the other end—the exact opposite of not wanting to change, where the person alters their behavior and changes without thought. When someone enters their life through something new, like a romance, a job, an addition to your family, etc., they allow it to consume them. They go out of their way to do everything the new person wants, never considering the impact on everything else. Not good. First of all, it's bad for the receiving party in that they can't respect someone that appears to have no backbone, and it gives them the impression it's acceptable to expect this from anyone. Second, the grand giver obviously hurts their own self by ignoring all of their own needs. Third, everyone else is neglected, which may cause people to resent the martyr or worse, abandon them. Harmful all around!

The person that changes drastically without thinking has made assumptions about how they should behave, either through what they've observed or heard in the past. It's never good to imitate to get through something, especially to get through a change. If there is no thought as to who they are and who they want to be, it will make everyone uncomfortable. All will sense something is "not quite right." This person has surrendered their entire self and will make themselves and those around them miserable.

The solution in either case? Change. Reprioritize. Balance. Try it out! As life presents new and wonderful challenges and opportunities, dig in! Appreciate yourself enough to allow you to try new ways, to give up old behaviors, and to indulge in wonderful new behaviors. The new activities may teach you something huge about yourself, and about a happy life. Decide what is important now, even if it's completely different than what you thought was important yesterday, and make a space between, not on top of, other priorities. It may not come to you overnight, or even in the first few tries, but if you stay flexible, you'll figure it out. Some big things to remember:

1) Kids that you are responsible for come first!
2) Allow yourself the time to get used to things, to grow and change, and acknowledge what you like about your new self!

3) Stay flexible when things don't flow the way you want, learn from it and try something different next time.
4) Balance time for you and for everyone around you that needs you. You don't need to give up either one to get the other; you can have it all!
5) Let go of things that are no longer important, either temporarily or permanently. Think through what and why you really need with pure honesty.
6) Realize that change allows you to grow and encounter more meaning in your life, which leads to a fulfilled heart and contentment. Let it in!

YOU ALWAYS HURT THE ONES YOU LOVE

Bad days happen, but you can still come out a winner.

Don't dump, splatter, or even flick any littlest piece of SH** on people you love, especially your family or significant other! Think about it. When all hell breaks lose and things are gloom and doom, the one thing you can count on is someone who loves and cares about you. When you have someone that sticks by you (maybe even when you don't deserve it), why would you try to talk them out of caring for you by dumping crap on them? The poor innocent bystander gets it, huh?

Might as well make it pure hell by pushing away the only people that can help, right? Oh, and there's a bonus! If you're crappy to them often enough, you will lose your appeal to them. They will may stop offering their help or concern, or even stop liking you! If you give them enough crap, you may even just drive them right out of your life! Cool, huh? Yeah, that's what you wanted, right? If it's not what you want, then why do it? Stop! Think!

I'm not telling you to suffer in silence or keep things from your loved ones. Not at all. I'm just saying they're not there to be your port-a-potty, conveniently there when you need to take a dump! You can share feelings about your troubles and bad days without covering those close to you with it! At a time that's considerate of your loved one, let them know what's going on, but be sure to thank them for listening. Be kind to them and let them know you appreciate them being there for you. Take the time to listen to them. They stopped to listen to you, didn't they? Even if you haven't found a time to throw a pity party in their presence, it's still not fair to fling a shovel-full of crap at them, just because they came in contact with you. Just the opposite is best. Express your gratitude towards their being there. Just that gesture alone will make you feel better.

You may be in a bad or sad mood. You may have just had somebody else dump a loader bucket of moist crap on you, barely leaving your head sticking out to breathe. It doesn't matter. As I've explained before, re-dumping this on someone else will never make you feel better, but dumping it on someone close to you is the ultimate offense. It tops the charts on things that make you feel especially guilty and poopy. If you ever do it unintentionally, just look at the hurt in their eyes or the disgust on their face and tell me, you aren't lower than low?

Caring people are there to let you vent, briefly, but only after you've made it clear you are not angry or upset with them. Be kind and considerate when you vent; it's really not that hard. If you've gone too far with your lack of control or the duration of your pity party, stop. Apologize, express your appreciation, and then ask them how they are doing. Focus on listening to how they are doing. Think about how crappy you would feel if you found out later that your loved one is bearing a much heavier load, but you were too selfish and self-consumed to stop and offer to help carry it? Moreover, you added more weight to their load, probably close to burying them in the pile. Does that make you feel great? Thought so.

Hard as things get sometimes, don't let the bastards get you down by stealing away the good things in your life. When you're with other people, check those crappy feelings at the door and savor the comfort and caring that's being shown to you. Give some comfort and caring back too, and see how that helps you through those bad things. Even a very little helps. Every little gesture and smile helps. Smile whenever you can.

If you've been a repeat dumper on your loved ones, this is not meant to make you feel bad about that. On the contrary, this is to make you realize you can turn it around, right this second! Stop dumping on them immediately and start scraping off any thing you or anyone else has piled on. Every positive, kind gesture out-weighs the bad ones about ten times over. If they've hung by you this long, it's probably all they are waiting for. I'll give you a couple of ideas.

Let's say you've had a horrid day and are just getting home. Instead of stomping in the door all crabby-looking and complaining, think before you even open that door. Leave the crap the world threw at you outside. Take a deep, cleansing breath and let it all flow out of your head. Be grateful and glad to see whoever joins you at home. Give them a hug—a real hug—and tell them it's good to be with them. Take care of these important things first, before you even think about discussing any of the negativity of the day.

Or let's say a friend or loved one calls you at work, but you're incredibly busy and stressed. You can't absorb anything they're saying because your head is already packed full and ready to explode. Tell them you're sorry you're so busy and can't talk long; ask them if you can catch up to them later when you can give them more attention. Either way, try to give them a minute of your time, and if it's someone you love on the other end, make sure you tell them so before you hang up. A high-stress moment can be instantly lessened if you let a small, pleasant interruption do its job. The person on the other end might just be one of the things that make your life worthwhile and make you feel good, so shouldn't they have priority over something that's making you feel awful?

Just a little more about those crappy days. Remember that we are only human and sometimes, we will have a "bad" day. Sometimes we're just too distracted with situations, events or things going on with out loved ones to focus on how we want things to be. Sometimes others do things and sometimes things happen that throw our world into a tizzy. Sometimes this happens. Once you've had a taste of perfect days and realize you have a lot to do with creating them, like I do, it seems to be very difficult to accept the occasional bad days, as it can make you feel like a failure. It's okay; we are not perfect, as hard as we try.

Whenever a crappy day hits you, don't be too hard on yourself. Do your best to stop and change your focus and mood, and hopefully, change your day. If you struggle or are just too tired, frustrated, or overwhelmed, again, don't be so hard on yourself. Try to be productive in a positive way, as much as you can, so you at least feel like you didn't waste the entire day. Even picking one small task to complete will help. Concentrate on being nice to those around you, because it could be very easy to lash out or let the SH** roll downhill on to others in times like this. But remember, it'll only make it worse for you.

Lastly, remember that today is today, and tomorrow is tomorrow, and tomorrow will not be today. It's a different day altogether and can be quite different. When you lay down in bed at the end of a crappy day, thank God for getting you through it, be proud of yourself for doing the best you could, and replay the day in your head, only replace what didn't go so well with how it would have been, had it been perfect, and ask for that tomorrow. Be thankful for the good days and fall asleep thinking about a great tomorrow and all that it entails, knowing you will wake up to a brighter, happier day.

BE KIND!

You truly never know a person's heartaches or struggles, so please, just be kind.

People need people, so most important of all, be kind to others, no matter what. No, I don't live in a fantasy world. I am painfully aware of what seems to be the "normal" behavior out there. It's typical for people to be rude, disrespectful, unhelpful, short-tempered, and snobby. It's unreal to me that some people just don't seem to think at all, anymore. Anyone with a soul would be appalled by it if they were ever forced to watch a video tape of them, replaying their typical day, don't you think? It's so sad.

Our natural reaction, to protect ourselves, may be to treat an unfriendly person in the same manner they are treating us. When you do treat them as you think they deserve, you drop to their level, add to the SH** pile, and accept and encourage that kind of behavior. Bad and more bad! So, I'm asking you not to imitate the negative behaviors. Break the pattern!

Besides having higher standards for yourself, you never know what other people have been through or are going through. High stress will make a person behave in very uncharacteristic ways. They can be so overwhelmed with stress and worry that all of their energy is focused on survival of the present day.

In this mode, it's nearly impossible to have any room for anything or anyone else. Whether they can explain or even understand their state is not important. People have to rely on each other in challenged times like this; it is your responsibility to try your best to be compassionate and as flexible and understanding as possible, just on the mere chance that this person may be dealing with something very difficult, and they are doing their best, under their circumstances. You'll never regret being the bigger person and being kind, even if you never know why someone is being unpleasant. At the end of the day, you can rest easy, knowing that you rose above, instead of adding to the SH** pile.

PEOPLE ARE SUPPOSED TO HELP PEOPLE!

You have no right to judge and condemn those in need by refusing to help them.

"I have a hard enough time making ends meet. Why should I work harder, just to give money to people that are too lazy to work?" Ouch! Another horrible excuse that hurts some of the most deserving people the worst! Are you really that cold? What if something like the following happened to you?

You and your spouse move across the country, away from family and friends, for you to take a high-paying job that you're quite proud of. You are living the good life, with a big house, fancy car, and luxury everywhere you turn. There's no need save for retirement yet. You have a lot of years to do that. Life is good. Then, the dark clouds overshadow you. The company is hurting and lays you off, just when unemployment is high. You apply for several jobs, but the competition keeps you from landing one. Other people are willing to get paid much less, but you can't afford your mortgage if you take less. Your spouse is willing to apply for jobs, but hasn't been feeling so great lately. After several doctor visits, your spouse learns they are dying of a deadly disease, and may only have months to live.

Your priorities turn from finding work to finding all possible (and expensive) treatments for your spouse. Their health declines quickly, and you spend all of your time caring for your spouse and trying to pay the bills that are threatening to remove every day necessities, including your home. You didn't have health insurance because you lost your job, and you never thought about buying life insurance. The treatments for your spouse are maxing out any credit you have. Things are bad, and you can barely deal with the emotion side of things. You have no support, as all of your family and friends are on the other side of the country. Even if you could ask someone for help, the financial debt is much too high to do any good. There is no hope.

A few months later, your spouse looses the battle after spending most of their last days in an expensive facility. You are heart-broken and wish you could have gone with them. What is there to live for now? You go through the motions necessary for your spouse's funeral and the legal changes necessary, but are so distraught in just a shell of a body. The house is foreclosed on, of course, and you have no choice but to claim bankruptcy. You don't know why you should even go on; the pain is too much to bear. You have no one to talk to, and nowhere to go. You find a little escape in drinking alcohol; at least it helps you to sleep and forget about everything for a while. Before you know it, you're one of those winos sleeping on the streets that always disgusted you. You don't care. You have nothing. You have no one. No one cares.

Could it happen? Does it happen? ABSOLUTELY! You're lying to yourself, if you don't think so. Maybe it's inconceivable to you because you have a ton of family and friends around you, and always someone to help you. Not everyone is that fortunate, though. Some have lost their family or have had to leave their family because they were abused or neglected. Some have experienced tragedies that they are unable to deal with, and they are unable to function. Some take a wrong turn and unintentionally become addicted to drugs or alcohol and live for their next fix. Some have mental or physical handicaps that do not allow them to take care of themselves. They have no control over their life. They hate it, but they cannot overcome it. This is very real. This is very common today.

The problem is, we all use an excuse of a stereotype of poor or homeless being equivalent to lazy. Guess what? There are lazy rich people too, but we don't stereotype them! There are lazy people in all levels of life, but that doesn't give us a reason to neglect people that need our help! There are plenty of poor, homeless, and desperate people that had absolutely no control over how they got there. It may have come from abandonment, abuse, neglect, brainwashing, war or disaster, unfortunate events, illness, financial misfortune, crime, or victimization, just to name a few. Do you think those victims have a choice? Most likely, no. What if it happened to you? What if you were desperate and no one helped. What if instead, they just called you lazy and were disgusted by you? What if people justified not helping you, by saying that some of their money might go towards someone that is lazy, and they can't take that risk? So for one lazy person, 10 victims have to suffer? Who are you to make that judgment on them?

Consider this: If everyone shared just one thing they could easily spare, many things could be very different in the world today. It tears me apart, how the world seems to have no heart, and worse yet, the lessons that go unlearned. One little thing can sometimes change or save a life, yet everyone's in a rush. Some think they can justify not helping because their life is so tough; they forget someone always has it worse and still needs their help. They inflict a tremendous amount of damage and hurt by ignoring and doing nothing. Ignoring doesn't make you not guilty of hurting someone, especially when you could have easily helped them. You are guilty of hurting people, when you ignore a chance to help them.

People act blind and have forgotten how to be kind, telling themselves they don't have a dollar to spare. Come on! Most of us really DO have a dollar to spare, and that dollar does make a difference. Think of what happens if ten million people (or much more) each parted with that precious dollar to help someone else. That's $10 Million Dollars! So you still don't think that can make a difference?!

So people are just too busy minding their own life, and don't realize the strife others are going through. Just a little understanding could ease so much pain. When people don't help others, they are sentencing those in need to further pain. But I wonder, how is it that these busy people have time to judge those in need? Who did they consult with to research how this person came upon this state of helplessness? And why are those that could help blaming the person in need, anyway? This is truly what happens when we refuse to help. We blame them and sentence them. I challenge you to understand that no matter the circumstances, your assistance will only help them, and along with that, benefit you as well.

When something "bad" happens to us, we typically feel sorry for ourselves and wonder what we did to deserve it, and when people don't understand our agony, we wonder how they can judge us, as they don't even know the circumstances. Don't you think that people in need have these thoughts constantly? How dare we judge them! Stop judging and take the time to help them, in any way you can, with a dollar or a kind word or help of any kind at all! You will never regret helping someone, and no matter the outcome, you still win through all the ways it benefits you, and your search for a happy life.

BIG PEOPLE ARE SUPPOSED TO TAKE CARE OF LITTLE PEOPLE

 **Act your age and take care of your children.**

It saddens me when I hear or see people acting as though their very own children are a burden to them. I'm not talking about the occasional complaint about a misbehaving child. I'm talking about the people that resist giving up their luxuries to accommodate their very own children's needs. Their thinking is so diluted that they think the outside, material conveniences are what will make them happy. They don't get that anything done out of love will bring them the fulfillment they're looking for, not the material things.

There's no purer love than that of a child, especially towards their parents. Children are a precious gift that brings an unimaginable amount of joy to anyone around them. All they require is someone to love them and to care for them. That duty is the direct responsibility of anyone in the child's life, yet some adults attempt to neglect all of it, and miss out on one of the most fantastic things you can do in your life.

I know we're all human, so I see how it happens, especially with new parents. The once very affectionate couple is no longer a couple, but a family, and the romance begins to sour. The baby requires love and attention too; love and attention that used to belong exclusively to the significant other. Silly as it may be, close-minded, selfish thoughts often cause one or both of the former couple to take this personally. This starts a snowball effect of hurt feelings from lack of attention or understanding, stress and exhaustion, resentment, and other negative feelings, all because one or both of the couple isn't thinking this through. The tiny little being is helpless, and not there by their choice. It was the couple that went through the motions that brought this little being into the situation, right? So it's the parents' responsibility to give this tiny human all the care, love, and attention he or she deserves. And I'll be honest, 99% of the big humans bringing about the creation of a little human have no clue how much care, love, and attention is required. Until you are a parent, and a parent that contributes greatly to the raising of a small being, you do not know the extent of it! (Trust me on that one, if you are considering going through any actions that could cause another being to be created! You need to be completely committed to giving your life to any tiny beings you create, or you should not be going through the act of creating one!)

Remember, we are the big people and they are the little people. Big people are supposed to help little people. It's that damn simple, and even animals know how to do it. So when you are responsible for caring for a younger being, think about things before you make any quick judgments or motions towards resenting anything about the situation. If you or your significant other is taking care of the child, naturally, there will be energy, attention, and time directed away from other things. The scary thing is, some grown-up idiots really think that love and attention given to a child somehow diminishes the "pot" of love and attention that is left for them. How ridiculous is that?

Moreover, there is often jealousy involved when the mere act of taking care of a child forces the caregiver to choose sometimes. Choices will need to be made to do what is best for the child. That could involve giving up some of the things the caregiver could do before, including staying up late at night to give their significant other some affection. The caregiver must make the choice as to where to use their energy and probably, to sleep when the baby is sleeping, so they can care for the baby when he or she is awake. This is a fact, not an intentional choice for the couple to be less caring towards each other.

The ideal way to care for a small being is to have the couple work together, equally, whenever possible, to avoid exhaustion and stress. Moreover, the couple needs to understand that the love between them does not go away as you add another being to love. With love and all other good things, there is no limitation or set quota; there is more than you can imagine available to everyone. The couple only needs to understand that whenever life changes, you need to be understanding of the changes.

"Us" means us—you and at least one other person TOGETHER, planning, making choices, etc. These things should be done as a unit, together, as it probably affects both of you. For example, take housework issues. Often times, the woman of the house feels overwhelmed with all the housework. Then, when the man of the house has time to help, he decides on his own to go golfing or hunting. That's a "me" decision and it leaves her feeling stranded, betrayed, hurt, and eventually, resentful. It goes directly against the "us" bond that is supposed to be in place.

"Us" will also include any others, such as children that you bring into the world or have any responsibility for. This includes any children that you may not have planned for. If you made the choice to pursue the action that creates another human being, you also made the choice to become part of an "us" at that time, both with the child and the other parent of the child! This is a very serious example of how a choice you make can impact the world!

Now, if you did bring a child into the world, you must make accommodations and changes in your life to serve the "us" before the "me." Even if you and the other parent do not get along, the child needs to come first. So suck it up and find a way to have civil communications with the other parent, as required to give that child what they deserve. After all, it was YOUR choice that brought them here, not theirs. They are entitled to a fantastic, loving life, and it's your obligation to do all you can to give this to someone that you created.

A simple adjustment to thinking and doing according to the "us" instead of the "me" is all it takes. You're not losing yourself or your luxuries; you're gaining harmony, fulfillment, and additional joy and love. Through it, you can experience the amazing feeling and the whole purpose of people needing people, which shines brightest in a child's eyes. They deserve the best you can give, and in return, you will receive one of the most amazing gifts of this life. I challenge you to find anything in this world to compare to the pure love children give, so freely and willingly, especially to those that care for them.

DO YOU HAVE ANY CHILDREN IN YOUR LIFE?

 **Children are a precious gift. Anything we do has a major impact on who they become.**

If you have any children in your life, do you realize they are the most significant and fulfilling things you can ever do with your life? I challenge anyone to convince me otherwise.

If you do not have any children in your life yet, please consider the following before you take any actions that may possibly result in the creation of another human being. Also, think about it before you interact with anyone with a child's state of mind. They are the most delicate and vulnerable minds of the universe. Think I'm being too dramatic? I wish.

Consider this: Children do not have the life experiences adults have to know that some people are warped. Children only know real feelings. Honest feelings. If someone is mean to them or neglects them mentally or physically, the child is convinced they are undeserving of being treated otherwise. They have no concept of the neglector's behavior coming from their own personal issues. The damage to their self-worth is often irreversible. Always be conscious of how you behave around children; they are little sponges drawing off of anything and everything we do. They cannot distinguish the bad from the good. They have to take it all in.

And worse, the single, most important thing to a child is acceptance and love from their parent or parent-figure. They yearn to spend time with the people closest to them. It's only natural, just like the baby animals you see, trailing after their mothers. Children NEED POSITIVE ATTENTION and LOVE from their parents more than any other thing in life.

If you have or are considering having children, PLEASE realize what a huge commitment it is. It WILL change your life. It WILL change your lifestyle. If you are a good parent, you WILL make many sacrifices for your offspring…that's just part of it. If you are not willing to put yourself behind your children, then you should never have children.

It makes me ill when I see parents resenting their children because of the time, money, and sacrifices that are needed. How stupid can people be? Did that child ASK to be born? NO! That child is an innocent victim of someone that just didn't take the few brain cells to think through what it means to bring another human being into the world. People that feel their children are a burden are obviously not doing their job. If they were expressing their love to the child, the positive feedback they'd receive would make them realize they've been blessed with a precious gift, and never feel so selfish again.

Having a positive affect on a child's life, whether they are your own or someone else's (who may not be providing the attention and love the child deserves) is one of the most important and rewarding things you can do. If you haven't experienced this wonderful feeling, please try it out. The love you get back is incredible; children are not afraid to give love back, unconditionally. It's a shame we become tainted by all the SH** in life and forget how to do this, all too soon.

Whenever you have the chance, don't allow the SH** to swallow up the children. Divert it, for their sake. It's the adult's job to protect the young; animals are capable, so shouldn't we be too?

Moreover, I firmly believe that it is EVERY adult's responsibility to be a good role model to ANY children in their life, and even any children they come across. Think of it this way. The definition of "ADULT" is that you have matured through the "CHILD" stage of life. Therefore, you should not act like a child when it comes to responsibility. Moreover, wouldn't you agree with me that the ADULT is there to nurture the CHILD?

What I'm saying here is that adults are responsible to children in regards to the two things every child needs the most: acceptance and guidance. Doesn't matter what the age of the child is—it applies throughout childhood—even as far as the 20's, and depending on who you are (like a parent) it may apply throughout that entire person's life! I don't know about you, but I still enjoy a pat on the back from my parents and a kind word of advice, every now and then.

This also applies to anyone who's interacting with anyone younger than they are, including children talking to younger children. Don't you agree, it's the least you can do for the sake of the future of the world? Yeah, I know that sounds dramatic, but that kid isn't going to stay a kid forever. Eventually, they will grow up and they will have an influence on the world as well.

I think people need to realize that they affect all people they interact with and that they have a stronger influence on them if the person is much younger. This younger person may be your child (and you already know my feelings on your obligation there), but the obligation is nearly the same if you choose to be with someone that has a child, especially if you're living with them. Realize though, that you also have an obligation for the rest of the younger people you come across—whether it's the paperboy, a neighbor, a relative, or even a stranger that happens to be observing something you're doing. It's all the same. You can have a tremendous impact on helping them decide who they are.

Again, don't feed them SH**, people! Give them only good stuff!

BELIEVE IN SOMETHING – NO WEAK EXCUSES ALLOWED

Not believing invites weakness and the inability to handle daily struggles.

Let's say you don't even believe God exists, and you make it known to people you come across, because you don't want to look like a foolish, weak person. I'm sure you have your reasons, but if you're sure about this, I just want you to take a minute and think about the following idea. Thinking with an open mind is always good, right?

When you die, you die alone. There will be no audience where you're going—no one to come back and tell everyone back here that "you were right." At that point, it's just you and your Maker. Someone did come up with the whole idea of how you could come to be (how you were conceived), after all. That someone will be there when you die, too, I'm pretty sure. Boy, I'll feel sorry for you when you die, if you're not right?

Let's say that your excuse is, you believe it's only luck that controls what happens. Okay, but that doesn't mean God isn't there, too. People do control most of what happens to them. God gives humans free will. They make their own choices how they live their life, how they treat other people, and what to believe. He'll never force it on anybody, and that's not what I'm trying to do here. I can tell you from my own life experiences that if you try to be a good person (by His definitions of treating others as you would truly like to be treated) and you really know what you want, focus on it, and believe and pray, that things will go "your way" more often than not. But you'll never know till you try it for yourself. Let me remind you, that if you do this skeptically or half-heartedly, you will get only partial results. God knows how you really feel.

Or, maybe you don't believe in all the miraculous things the Bible talks about, and you're sure about evolution. Again, it doesn't mean God doesn't exist. Why wouldn't God use things that He created in the world to get to His end goals? And if He tried to explain it all, would we really be capable of understanding it? I doubt it. So, He did his best to give us stories and people in the past to explain what we could possibly comprehend. I don't think some of the literal details are always interpreted exactly as He meant it; people get all hung up on those details, saying, "Oh, that could NEVER happen!" I think that's a total waste of time. I think we need to remember that our small minds are probably not interpreting everything as completely as it really is.

So am I saying I don't believe there were miracles? Absolutely not. I DO believe there have been many miracles in the past and that they do happen every day. Just because you don't see lightning and hear a booming voice from the sky, it doesn't mean a miracle didn't happen. I believe God uses other people, situations, nature, and angels to perform these miracles. I believe that most of the time, we're too caught up in our small-mindedness and life's business to even notice them. Maybe some people can see them and others can't, based on how much faith they have or even what God chooses. I don't know, and again, it's not important for me to know. All I know is that as a child, my mind was open to this, thanks to loving parents that shared their beliefs with me. Perhaps that's what has allowed me to notice some of the miracles in my life; with each one, my faith grows. I consider myself very fortunate, and wish everyone could experience the comfort and peace that is gained when you believe. If you're a parent, don't deprive your children! Let them know God is there! Why set them up for a life of loneliness and struggles? Don't you want them to have a happy life?

I want to go back to my point on not taking the Bible literally, all the time. I really don't care if Adam and Eve (the very first people) were a form of an ape, cavemen, or human form like we are. I really don't care if Adam and Eve were even their real names—it doesn't matter. What matters is the Bible story that God is trying to present. My interpretation of their story is simply this: There were two people that chose not to listen to God, thereby proving that people were not prepared for the complete paradise that God intended. This is the reason we must live in this world until we fully understand what God has enabled us to be, and what He wants us to have. Only then will we reach paradise, or heaven.

God wrote this story and many others to teach us. He tried to put it in simple terms, so we would understand. If you make bad choices during your life in this world, and you're not truly happy, it determines where you go next. Maybe you go there permanently, but then again, maybe you just come back to this world, over and over, until you finally get it. Maybe God chooses, but I think more likely, we choose for ourselves. I don't know, and I honestly don't care. To me, it's a no-brainer. You live your life based on where you want your life to go, and go from here. Perhaps heaven, hell, and purgatory are all in the present, and ways to describe how you feel today? Either way, I prefer paradise, both today and when it's my time to go, and I would like everyone I care about there too. I pray for strength and try every day to be a better person than I was the day before. I don't know about you, but I really appreciate people I meet that get this. They are a joy to be around.

Perhaps you don't believe because something awful has happened to you or someone you care about. Your defense is, "If there is a God, why would He let this happen?" First off, I need you to know I feel deeply sorry for the burden or the tragedy you are enduring or have endured. I admit, there doesn't seem to be any fairness in this world, sometimes. But I need to tell you I don't think God is responsible. God's vision of our home is paradise or heaven, not a world with hardships. As I mentioned earlier, people's free will creates the world we live in. The more bad behavior that occurs, the more bad things we'll see in the world. Good behavior is the only thing holding it back completely. I admit, sometimes I think evil is winning in this world, but it's no reason to join the team. In the end, I know good will prevail—good is always stronger than evil. The problem with this world, I think, is that there's a higher volume of people making bad choices than there are people making good choices.

In the end, I don't have to live with it. I plan to live in, and to go to, a better place, if my behavior over the course of my life makes me deserving of it. Also, I've noticed that the better I behave, the more people around me think before they do things. They see I'm happy with my life, and pay attention to what I'm doing. I'd rather have this influence on people, and not be someone that people identify as bad, trouble, negative, and unhappy. (You notice how easily all those words go together?)

Also, you need to know that evil is attracted to weak and hopeless situations, because it can be very easy for evil to influence anyone in this situation to curse God and to behave badly, in anger or hurt. I think evil will always lean towards someone with doubt (an easy target) versus someone that actively prays and stays close to God, obviously because they tend to be more easily persuaded. I found that at the points in my life when I was terrified, when my heart was breaking, and even once when I might have died briefly, I naturally asked God for help and I received it immediately. Along with it was Him telling me everything was going to be all right, so that I was at peace, instantly. This allowed me to comfort anyone around me, despite my burden.

My advice is to stop any habits you have on becoming angry with situations and replace it with just talking to God for help and direction. The more you do it, the more you'll see how effective this is. Moreover, you won't be a burden to other people; you might even be able to help them, which will give you a whole different feeling of contentment, no matter what's going on.

If you want to build your strength in living a good life and in warding off evil stabs at you, it's very easy to do. Praying, through formal prayers or just talking to God about anything is the first step. Making choices that are best for you and other people and choosing with your heart and out of love, versus choosing out of fear is the next step. If you need guidelines, there are the 10 Commandments, the Beatitudes, and the Bible to reference. Hanging around good people will also help because you'll have real examples. Then, it's time to make a very easy commitment to this type of lifestyle. There are many churches out there—some good, some not so good, I admit--but a good one is there to help give you guidance and help you to expand your faith, at least once a week.

Oh, there are a million excuses why people don't take this step. "I don't have time." "I don't like that church or that pastor." "We were forced to go to church when I was a kid." "It's too long." "I don't like the way they carry on." "I don't like how they ask for money." "I don't like all the bad people that go there and act like they're all that." "I don't get anything out of it." Wow. All I can say is, weak, weak, weak! (Excuses, that is.) Let me show you how weak these excuses are.

First of all, if you spend even one hour a week watching TV, sitting online talking smack to your friends, or doing anything else unnecessary, don't even try to tell me you don't have time. I happen to know that God watches over us 24 hours a day, 7 days a week. One hour a week to go to church doesn't usually kill me. There are many churches in my area with a wide offering of services on both Saturday and Sunday. If I make it a priority (that is, go to church before I do something else that can wait that hour) it's really not that hard to get there every week.

Next, if you're going for the other people that are there (pastor or parishioners), stay home. That's the wrong reason to go! Your reason for going needs to be to talk to God, to thank Him, and to listen to His message during that service. Period! If you don't want to associate with anyone else in the church, then don't! Go in, go out, and don't talk to anyone but God, and they'll never know who you are. If it's hard to tolerate the soloist that can't hit a note and goes on and on, well, tell God you're going to ignore her and just talk to Him, in your mind, while she's singing. She has the right to pray however she pleases, and so do you. If you are tolerant of other people, it only helps you grow. If you're too wimpy to do this, then find another church.

Money. While some churches might try to make you realize an obligation to give to the needy (including the church, to pay the bills), no one is making you pull out your wallet when you walk in the door. You can pass on giving anything, forever if you wish. If you do give just so people won't look at you, again, you're doing it for the wrong reason! Giving is something that God teaches we should do, and rightly so. If each of us that could spare a little something helped the unfortunate, the world would be just fine. (Seriously, think about a billionaire that throws a million at an orphanage or a third-world country charity! What an impact it would make!) But, again, people don't always choose to give when they can. I can only tell you that whenever I have given something (even when I wasn't sure I could completely pay my bills), somehow, my bills always got paid. Very often, I later received money from somewhere I didn't expect it—a refund on an insurance discount, a gift, or a raise. My point is, give a little, if you can. You'll never regret it. God teaches that you'll always receive more back than you give, and I believe it. Personally, I don't give substantial amounts to the churches I attend. I give them some, but save my big donations to help starving children. That's just my preference. You are free to donate, or not donate, whenever you choose.

Don't get anything out of attending services? Gee, whose fault is that? How old are you now? Do you understand that it's your responsibility to take what you want out of any event you experience? Drag your butt there and just try to listen to the words of one of the prayers. Try to listen to the readings and sermons to see if you can learn just one thing from it. (Or more common, to remind you of something you already knew, but don't pay enough attention to!) Just take about an hour to stop and think and breathe. If you do any of these things, you won't feel like it's a waste of your time. You'll only get out of it what you put in to it. You'll never cease to be surprised how far you can go with an open heart.

I'm sure there are other reasons (or excuses, as I call them) as to why people don't believe, to which I think we can apply this simple fact. What you put into your life and your own growth feeds into the type of life you have. Don't blame anyone for your life, if you don't put your heart into it; you'll only get back what you put in. I realize there are more valid reasons for not attending a weekly service, but do your best to try to get there. For people with children, they may think it's too hard because most kids I know will not sit still and be silent for an hour. Consider this. God knows how much effort you put in to getting to services. You get bonus points for packing up the kids and hauling them to church. Besides, God loves the innocent children, so bring them in! Even with all the wiggling, you should still be able to focus on a piece of a prayer or the sermon. And how on earth will your children understand the importance of believing in something if you never expose them to it?

They will tend to imitate your behavior, you know. No matter how the adventure to church with a squirmy kid or two ends up, you still get credit for trying! For those physically unable to get there, if you're able to watch TV, turn on a channel with a service or even one of the religious channels, at least for a little while. If you are able to hold the Bible or other religious book, read! Do what you can—you'll never regret it. For me, it's an easy choice. I like peace, harmony, happiness, and success for myself and the people around me, so I choose to believe in God and do the best I can.

WHY ARE YOU AFRAID TO BELIEVE?

Don't want to believe? Perhaps you don't want to take responsibility for yourself.

Why do some people cling to being non-committed to belief in the good things, like the power of free will, heaven, and a greater being like God, or any grander existence than what we know in our current life? Are they afraid of it? Are they afraid they have to be good? Is it because they don't want to be responsible to themselves or to others? Do they think they're following the crowd and being cool, and therefore, don't want to be different? I hate to be the one to tell them, but non-believers are the minority, not the majority. And if it's popularity they're going for, we need to remember that you make yourself less popular when you imitate behavior, instead of doing what you really wanted to do. People don't think more of people that follow the crowd—they think less of them. Don't you naturally think less of someone that has no backbone? Well, so do others.

Not choosing to believe, a non-believer makes a weak and easy target to too many negative thoughts, situations, and behaviors, which only makes their life worse. The sadness in this is again, that each person chooses this. God and free will waits for the moment (no matter how few and far between) when we choose to believe. You have to believe in good things to ever reach a state of heaven, whether here, during your life on earth, or after when your body dies and you change form and move on to whatever's after this "life." You decide.

Take back control of your life back and choose to believe. What have you got to lose? Again, if you won't believe in good things, you are basically pushing all good things away from you. Your free will and your choices, including the choice to not believe, leaves clear instructions that you want the opposite of good. There is no in-between. So what do you lose? Ultimately, you lose the state of heaven, whether it's here in the present, or after this life is over. If you don't believe in it, you cannot exist there because you are telling the universe that you do not want it. Free will grants your wishes. It's always your choice to go in the opposite direction of all that is good, if you wish. It's just not anywhere I ever want to go, and I don't want to take the slightest risk of ending up in hell, again, whether it's in the present, or when my body expires.

Did you just scoff at that statement? Don't believe me? Okay ponder this, then. Whenever you choose to do something, or believe something that cannot help you or your life, you are freely and actively choosing something that can only make your life worse. It's simple. You choose beliefs and things for your life to make it better or worse. One or the other—it can't be both.

So you're still going to argue that you wanted to choose to make it worse? That's just silly and I don't believe you. So my point once again: Think things through before you do them. Think a belief through before you choose not to believe it, or at least hope in it. If you're too lazy to do your own thinking, no problem. The negative forces will do it for you, and probably have been, for a good portion of your life. Take back your thinking. What have you got to lose? Just bliss. Just happiness. Just peace. But it's your choice.

When people choose not to believe in God or in the universe's ability to give them all things good, they push all of that away. So what's left? Well, the opposite of good, that's what. Life is very simple. It's all about choices. You choose one side or the other. Not choosing one thing is the same as choosing the opposite. There is no "on the fence." A deliberate choice to not choose something does imply and does invite the opposite. Think about your perception, when you ask someone, "Do you believe in God?" If they answer, "I'm not sure," you know they can't really believe, don't you? It really is that simple.

WHY AM I SO AFRAID OF MY SPIRITUALITY?

**God = Good. God = Peace.
Why wouldn't you want that?**

Why am I so afraid to explore God and spirituality? Is it because I will discover that I am the only one to blame? Am I so confused that I blame everything and everyone for the frustrations and discomforts and pain in my life, yet I do nothing to help myself pursue peace? It's so easy to blame someone else for things we're not happy about. I suppose it's human nature and a way of protecting myself from my own worst enemy…me. Many of us blame God and use it and an excuse for not seeking Him out. How sad.

Do yourself a favor and ponder this for just 5 minutes out of your busy life. The REAL TRUTH is that God loves each one of us so much that He created us to decide what we want to be and how we want our life to be. It's not up to Him. It's up to ME. I'm not talking about the decision to "handle" whatever life gives me. I'm talking about ME being responsible for clearly defining what I want my life to be. For ME making my life what I want it to be.

I hammer on these basics throughout this book, over and over, but I'll do whatever it takes to remind me and possibly to get it through to you, that my clear definition and thoughts about my life MAKE IT what it IS. I'm sure God cries daily as He watches us think negatively and constantly cause ourselves unnecessary hardship and pain. He has tried to tell us, over and over, but most of us refuse to listen. We refuse to take responsibility for ourselves and then, blame it on Him or someone else. So unfair.

With God comes all things good, so why do we ignore that He's there? Why do we spend precious time idling on negative, worrisome, exhausting, self-defeating thoughts and activities? That time could be spent learning more about God and thus, learning more about ourselves. It would be so easy to take just a couple of hours a month away from doing something that will not improve your life to change things. We could watch a DVD, read, attend anything, or engage in any activity to further explore God and all the amazing things He wants to offer you. You could change your life. Please ponder this a little while longer. You could change your life. It's all too easy to coast through life, muddled in fear of why we shouldn't pursue the truth about what God wants for each and every one of us. We don't even know what we fear or we would admit we can only benefit from pursuing God.

He commands that each of us chooses our own life; He only wants us to be happy. Blaming the rest of the world for our unhappiness only moves us farther from the truth. The unbelievable thing is, the truth is at our fingertips, each and every moment of each and every day, yet we push it away for fear we might have to take responsibility for ourselves. But truly, isn't this the exact thing we all want—control over our lives? It's right here! It's always been right here!

There are endless ways to pursue God and His truth. He has blessed us with so much guidance. You can choose whatever you prefer. Movies, magazines, books, radio, internet, speakers, community gatherings, formal services, friends and family, seriously, whatever you prefer! Personally, I really enjoy movies or audio books written specifically by people that were inspired to share their life-changing events and guidance as they discovered the truth or the secret about how God allows us to create our own life. It leaves me with such a peaceful, uplifting, hopeful attitude that even strangers seem to seek me out. Imagine how this feels, to be without worry, fear, or negative thoughts, even for a little while. It's pure heaven!

The more you pursue or indulge, the longer and stronger the feeling. And as it was meant to be, as you feel this way, it spills over onto those around you, in some shape or form. As you give, you receive, most times in much greater magnitude than what you gave. All of this continues to build, strengthen, and lead you closer to peace, regardless of what may be happening around you.

This is the truth and it is waiting for each of us to embrace. The length of time it takes to acquire the truth is dependent on the effort put forth as again, God puts us in charge of our lives. If we turn away from opportunities to learn about it, the result can only be more time spent on things that will not improve our life. Fear and discomfort build, and we push the truth farther and farther away; we will never be truly happy without the truth.

The moment we realize that only we are to blame for our life, and only we dictate what we, and our life will be, we are reaching for the truth and will no longer fear getting to know more about how God only wants us to be happy. Remember, God's gift of free will puts us in charge of what we believe and what we want. If you choose to not really believe, you are ordering God and goodness to stay away from you. He cannot be in your life when you order Him to stay out. Remember, it's your deep-down feelings that control your life. Maybe, truly, you're on the fence and your fear keeps you from believing until you have some proof. That's fine, but have you asked for God to prove He's there, and really mean it? You have to really want it.

Review my "You are in Control" chapter to make sure your requests are clear and what you really want. Then, ask the angels to help you. Here's a simple prayer I learned when I was very young. If I could do it at 4 years old or so, you can too.

> Angel of God, my guardian dear
> To whom God's love commits me here
> Ever this day (night) be at my side
> To light and guard, to rule and guide.
> Amen.

He cannot be in your life or help you in any way unless you ask. You are the boss of this.

Reach for the truth. Reach for God. You have nothing to lose, and it WILL change your life. I challenge you to let God in and tell me He didn't change your life for the better!

WHEN SH** COMES YOUR WAY, SIDE-STEP IT

Wading in SH will make you feel SH***Y.**

Grudges. Resentment. Jealousy. Revenge. I'm not gonna lie to you. SH** will flow your way, sometimes. People will wrong you. Things will not always go your way. SH** comes running around your toes, your ankles, or even all the way up to your neck, sometimes.

Don't let it pull you in! If you do, you'll sink right into it like quicksand, only it's much uglier, and a whole lot stinkier. It drowns you, and covers you with an icky layer. On the other hand, if you find a way to rise above it, you will feel success and shine like you never imagined.

Yeah, people will use you. People will take what you feel is rightfully yours. People will hurt your feelings. When something bad occurs, you have two choices. You can go along with the flow of the crap, floating down the river of SH** and give 'em what they really deserve. You can grow horns and one-up them with something even worse. You'll show them!

Guess what? What you're really doing is showing everyone that you are no better. You're a piece of poop, just like the person that wronged you. You belong in the same miserable world that they live in. You belong in the river of SH**. And honestly, that's what you'll feel like. It will not make you feel good. Oh, you may fool yourself into thinking that it'll make you feel good, temporarily, but it's really a lie. Deep down, you're not proud of yourself. I know you are probably angry or hurt, and would love to lash out. It's okay to acknowledge that. It proves you have feelings, unlike this other person. What's not okay, though, is letting that person control who you are or how you behave. You have to stay in control. You have to keep your dignity.

So what do you do? Well, if you can, walk away from the situation completely. Even when you run into that person, ignore them. Block out all bad karma from your view. Don't waste your energy on them. Everyone will notice, including them. It'll make them realize you are a step or two above them, and it might even make them stop and think. No promises there, but once in a while, it makes them realize they're not so cool. Personally, I feel sorry for mean people and view them as "emotionally handicapped" and very miserable with their life. How can they not be, since content people have no reason or desire to treat others badly, no matter what's going on. I thank God that I'm not miserable, like that person probably is.

Can't walk away? Okay. When you have to communicate with them, promise yourself you won't compromise who you are because of them. Only behave in a way you (and your momma) would be proud of. No matter what they do or say, stop and think, so you can side step their crap. You can be sarcastically nice, if worse comes to worse.

For instance, let's say you run into someone that totally used you, and you catch them watching you. Things get deeper, when this person approaches you and tries to talk to you, in a group of people. You give them a huge smile, and one-word answers. They continue to press you, and might even try to use you again, pretending they did nothing wrong.

Oh, this could really get to you, because they are completely insulting you and trying to use you again! Unbelievable! They may even bring up the uncomfortable topic. Here's the deal. You don't have to respond to them, but it feels better if you politely say something to let them know you don't have time for their kind. Even if they ask you a direct question, you do not have to answer them. You can choose to side step it.

With a huge smile on your face, just say something like, "Oh, you know what? I see someone I want to talk to. Have a REALLY good day!" This makes it very clear to them they can't make you go there, and that you don't want to talk to them. It also lets them know they didn't crash your world—you're still going about your business and socializing. Emphasizing the "really" can be taken many ways. And guess what else? If this person has an audience, or tries to bitch to someone about you, what can they say? Not a darn thing, can they? You did nothing wrong. You come out smelling like a rose. They take their SH** with them. Sweet.

SOMETIMES YOU NEED TO JUST SIT BACK, AND LET SH** GO!

Flow with the good stuff when it's there, but let the questionable stuff pass by.

As mentioned in another chapter, you don't always know all of the details that may be contributing to a bad situation. When you don't know all the facts, you can easily become very upset by someone's behavior or at a certain circumstance. Let me repeat this. You don't always know all of the information, so take it easy and sit back, if at all possible! When in doubt, save yourself the drama and don't take things personally. Let me give you some common examples.

    A. Someone says something extremely mean or rude to you.

If you have knowledge of some other possible factors, you would most likely discard their comments and not take it to heart. For instance, if you knew they had a mental condition or if you knew they were under severe stress at the time. Now unless you are a miniature, magical being that is capable of living inside that person's head, how would you know, for absolute certain, that such a circumstance does not exist? Even if you were capable of this, what if the person isn't even aware they have one of these conditions? It can and does happen to the best of us. Try to keep this in mind when someone is rude to you, and I guarantee the impact to you will be much less severe. What's the benefit in letting it get to you, anyway? Intentional or not, it's just SH** being flung at you. You're always better off to just lean back and let it fly by.

After raising a very moody teenage daughter, I strongly encourage you to consider any teenagers you know as having "severe stress" and to disregard any personal verbal attacks they may open with you. It is a very trying time for most kids as they try to figure out who they are, and they really don't mean to hurt you—they just need to shoot at the nearest target sometimes. If you don't put them in the "mentally unstable" category during those times, you can easily become more upset than you should. It is your job to stay calm and help them; you cannot do this if you take the harsh things they say to heart. Consider what they've said with a clear, factual method of thinking. If there is some factual weight to what they're saying, consider discussing a change with them. (But only if it keeps them safe and is best for them! Don't cave, trying to be the "cool" parent!) By the way, she is no longer a teenager and she is no longer moody. She outgrew both, once she allowed herself to think about things more, and it's wonderful to have her back!

Don't use your emotions to think about how rash, brutal, and disrespectful their comments are; remember they have a temporary mental condition—they are temporarily mentally handicapped. It's not going to help if you let these nasty comments get to you; you'll be instantly upset. And trust me, they don't realize how spiteful they are, at the time. They have higher priorities trying to figure out which way to go in life. If you stay cool and remind them you're doing what's best for them, once things have cooled down, they'll likely appreciate it some day. Teenage years, in my opinion, are a temporary period of insanity for most people, so please keep this in mind when you're dealing with one; cut them some slack. As always, don't let the SH** they're flinging at you every other minute stick to you, and don't add to their overwhelming pile. It will not go on forever.

    B. Something you do triggers a past experience someone else had, that left a bad memory in their mind.

In this case, they're not really upset with you, or possibly even your action, but rather, they're re-living a painful experience they once had. Again, any negative reaction they may have is directed at the pain, even though it may appear to be towards you. It's not intended for you, personally. They may be struggling with their own feelings and be unable to control what they throw your way. Better to be safe and just dodge it, rather than add to their pain. Again, they may or may not even be aware how badly it's affecting them, or even where it came from. Most people are not that in-tune with their thoughts and feelings, so don't be too hard on them.

C. You just met someone new and you really felt a connection, but they lose touch.

Even though you exchanged phone numbers or email addresses and expressed how eager you were to talk to them more, they never contact you, or cease communications shortly after. To your disappointment, they don't respond to your contact with them, either.

Before you go beating yourself up, thinking you must've said or done something wrong, stop! Before you label yourself as an undeserving loser, STOP! Again, you don't know the whole story. The possibilities are too many to list, but it's not the reason that's important anyway. I'll be honest with you. Most of the time, you will never learn why, so don't think about it longer than a second. Take the pleasant encounter for what it was—a pleasant encounter. Continue to look forward to any pleasant encounters you have, no matter how brief. It sure beats the crappy, unpleasant ones, doesn't it?

Not everyone we meet is meant to be in our life, or in our life forever. Be grateful for any positive interaction you have with anyone; don't focus on how you're needing more afterwards. Don't lose sight of the benefits of just having that time with that person. I'm sure that they enjoyed the experience as well. Just in case you're not getting this yet, let me give you some examples why you might not have heard back from the person:

- They were not honest with you about their availability, but just wanted to talk to you.
- They are going through a major life change (job, moving, relationship, illness) and just enjoyed

someone neutral where they didn't have to expose the hardship.
- They are hiding something else that's embarrassing (conviction, addiction, etc.)
- After getting to know you, they realize your standards are higher than what they're willing to live by and honestly know you deserve better (trust people if they tell you that you deserve better—they know who they are).
- Something serious has happened in their life. (Someone I know once became upset because a new guy friend didn't call for a week after she slept with him; after embarrassing herself with harassing phone messages, she learned his father had passed away the day after and he was out of town handling everything. Needless to say, he put her in her place and never spoke to her again.)

There are a ton of reasons someone just isn't ready for someone new in their life. When you're going through a major life change and struggling to find yourself, it really isn't fair or healthy to bring someone new into their life. Sit back and wait for that person to know what it is they want. If you are meant to be with them, they will come find you when they're ready. In the meantime, don't close yourself off from more new and great encounters.

To sum it up, don't create SH** unnecessarily. Do you really want to be with someone that's not pumped up to be with you anyway? Don't argue with me that they need to get to know you better; it's every person's right to choose who they get to know better. Don't take it personally and let them decide what is best in their life. You don't know all the underlying SH** and sometimes, it's just better off left alone. Enjoy positive interaction with people and let it go where it's meant to go. This is the flow you can dive into and bask in. As long as it's all good, go with it. The second it gets negative or you begin to smell the ugly scent, pull over and get out. Take your dignity with you.

LIFE WILL CHANGE—MAKE SURE YOU CHANGE FOR THE BETTER

Embrace change, don't fight it. It will help you reach fulfillment.

If you cringe or freak out at changes in your life, this chapter is for you. I hate to break it to you, but you do NOT have total control over everything that happens in your life. You can control you, but you cannot control the situations and people around you. You can only control you. Big or small, change means adjustment. Adjustment. Not the world crashing down, just an adjustment. The world isn't crashing down, after all. The ground is still there, beneath your feet, isn't it? The sky's still up there too, right? Okay then. The world is intact, so make sure you are too.

I'm not implying change is bad. Change is neither good nor bad—it is what it is. Change. How you adjust to it IS in your control. Your adjustment can make a negative impact or a positive impact. So tell me, what kind of adjustment and impact will make you feel best about any change in your life? You may think this is an easy answer, so I challenge you to take a good hard look at how you've adjusted to change so far. Was it really how you wanted to handle it? Now remember as you read on, the past is in the past. Learn from it and be wiser today and tomorrow. Leave everything that doesn't leave you with a happy memory behind.

We all encounter major life changes at some point in our life. It's inevitable; none of us can avoid it. That's what life does. It presents challenges and changes that teach us more about ourselves, and sometimes, about others. Whether the change involves people, events, a job, health, or finances, it's all the same. Life changes require some kind of adjustment because something is drastically different. Change is change, and we need to stay flexible and adjust in a way that we are happy with, in such a way that we are proud of. Be aware of the adjustment you are making and make sure it's what's best for you and the others impacted by it. So when change comes to you, take a moment to stop to focus on how you want things to be going forward, versus looking back and laboring over the change, or denying the change has occurred altogether. Negative thoughts about the past will only harm you, so keep your eyes on the future. Have faith, as most change I've seen brings something greater and grander into a life, when it is allowed to come about.

Let me start with a very common life change that all of us have ever experienced or witnessed. Two people fall in love and they get married. There's a lifetime of bliss in their future. At some point, they may start a family, and a change begins. The adjustment is immediate, as they start to plan and dream and stress out about conceiving or adopting, the pregnancy, and the wait. For some, the adjustment is not so easy, especially if things don't working out quite the way they envisioned. Even when things go as the couple thought it should go, the challenges and the unknown future starts to freak some people out.

Change is happening and an adjustment, along with it. It seems more common than not, people start to slip into a trance, thinking they suddenly need to become someone else. But no one trained them on how to play this new role. No one really explained what it would feel like, or how to act or how to handle it all. Even the smartest and most laid-back person feels completely lost, and can't even see the road. Perhaps the fear of responsibility makes them think they should be more stressed out and grumpy…that their days of "happy-go-lucky" and fun are gone. The party's over. Perhaps the mere struggle to figure out what to do next or handle it all consumes the mind beyond their control. Whatever the reason, an adjustment of the person's personality changes, too often, causing a very negative impact to their personality and to the environment around them. Unfortunately, the very person that once caused so much bliss, is stuck in that environment.

We've all seen it. The smiles and giggles disappear. The air around them is uneasy and uncomfortable. The slightest movement from either of the no-longer blissful couple causes major explosions. One or both are stifling any chance of happy occasions or any expression of contentment. How did they transport themselves from their personal paradise to bitter hell? Why do they resent everything the other person does? For most, it's a slow process and they've lost track of how it happened, and now, they're stuck. No glimmer of hope or chance of finding the road back out of there.

A negative adjustment. That's how it happened. And probably many negative adjustments—each one feasting off the one before. One or both have forgotten who they are, and in their turmoil, who their loving significant other is. In their freak-out over the changes that are occurring, they have betrayed their sacred bond. This is often enough to break their hearts and those of anyone witnessing it. Resentment sets in and all too soon, it seems too late to ever go back.

Let's walk through a possible situation in slow motion, to watch where negative adjustments have been used, for first-time parents:

1. The pregnancy doesn't happen as easily as they hoped. One or both are feeling inadequate and wondering if their significant other thinks they're not capable.

    Negative adjustment: Seriousness and worry are welcomed in.

2. They're finally pregnant and the reality of it all sets in. She probably isn't feeling very well and is tired all the time.

    Negative adjustment: She decides it's not fair that she is having to go through this sacrifice alone and wants to wipe the smile clean off of her partner's face. She makes it clear that if she's not having fun, neither can her partner in crime.

    Reactive adjustment: The significant other is perplexed about her personality change and doesn't dare discuss this while she's in this state;

all he can do is tiptoe around, snap to the orders, and try to keep her happy.

Subsequent reactive adjustment: The expecting mother knows her partner is not being his true self and is uneasy and unsure of their relationship, yet her misery occupies all her energy and she doesn't have anything left to be nice. Reactions go on an on, building a mountain of resentment over just a few months' time. No one remembers who they are. No one knows how to act.

3. The baby comes, and while there's joy in the environment, the nasty resentment and questionable personalities and relationship have intensified all emotions. It's a sensitive environment, despite having reached the end of a challenging phase. Another intense change has occurred, once again forcing an adjustment. Neither knows how to act as a parent. They are intimidated and defensive, and fear the other will sense their discomfort.

   Negative adjustment: Both distance themselves and distract the other by snapping at them over nothing.

   Reactive adjustment: Resentment, low patience, and trade-offs in place of the previous team effort.

   Subsequent reactive adjustment: Additional resentment and anger, especially if one parent seems to be handling the new situation.

4. At this point, the couple needs each other more than ever, but all the negativity between them has them both on the defense; they are both feeling stranded and alone instead of enjoying the closeness, joy, and strength of a family unit. More negative adjustments occur to survive.

This is just one very common example of how a series of negative adjustments and lack of communication can cause an incredible, misunderstood mess! Whatever the situation, all hope is gone for fixing it now. You feel like you can never get back to what it used to be. You're right—you can't. You will never get back to what they used to be, because so much has changed. That's the very definition of change. But I challenge you…why does anyone want "how it used to be?" Ultimately, don't we want "better than it used to be?" I do. So, now it's time to make some positive adjustments to ALL the changes. Both life event-introduced and self-inflicted changes. But where does one start?

The most obvious place is with one's self. In order to have a positive impact on someone else, you must first have positive feelings about who you are. If you lose yourself through changes that come your way, take a moment and find yourself again! You were born to be just uniquely you. No one else can even try to be you. That is your sole job on this earth—to be yourself and accordingly, to be true to yourself. Take a good hard look at who you were and who your significant other fell madly in love with. What is it that people really like about you that's different from everybody else? That's who you're supposed to be. If you fell into a "I think this is who I'm supposed to be or this is how I'm supposed to act" routine, snap out of it! You are cheating yourself and along with it, everyone around you! While certain responsibilities do require certain actions on your part, it doesn't mean you have to sway from being yourself! Who said relationships and kids and major life changes have to be serious and stressful? There's no rules on that! You want to be the best at a new role you have acquired? Just be yourself, and adjust for the better. Even if you have no clue what you're doing, be more loving, more gracious, more giving, more fun. You can't go wrong, then. No matter the situation, there's always room for that, and it will always have a positive impact on you and your environment. And remember, your environment is full of other people.

The people most touched by any adjustments you make are those that love you the most. (Thus the saying, "The closest target takes the bullet.") Remember, this includes your significant other. Even if you've spent months upon months at war, carefully watching your strategy and building up your armor and your ammunition, it's time to drop it all! What the hell? You actually forgot you are on the same team! Oh, there's your pride, you say. After all, you're in the right, you say? Okay, so let's give this an honest look. You're proud of being a jackass to the person that matters most to you? You're proud of continuing to pass the hurt back and forth because it matters at all who's right? When you're on the same team, does it matter who's right? It hurts the TEAM, so no, it doesn't matter who's right. When you made a commitment to become the couple, you vowed to do what's best for the team. Have you possibly lost sight of that? And if you have any children, they are now part of that team as well. First and foremost, it must be what's best for the team!

When you experienced states of bliss, it was because you were both on-board with the team concept. Your communications and your actions catered to keeping the team strong. Nothing could stop you or any of the dreams you had. Now, through a series of events, challenges, or changes, the color of your jerseys are masked by the armor of resentment and distress.

Drop the fricken armor—now! Be honest with yourself about who you really are and how you really feel about the rest of your team. It will take the team working together to overcome the hurdle you have created. Neither of you can do it alone. Provide strength and encouragement to each other to just be your true selves and you'll remember; nothing can get in your way.

Which team do you want to be on? Team Bliss or Team Alone? You can't be on both sides. You need to choose. So pick a team and play accordingly! And when you play, don't sit on the bench, letting the rest of the team do all the work and take all the hits. Get your butt in there and play hard for the team! It won't be back to the way it used to be. It will be oh, so much better! There will be more changes in the future, but sticking with positive adjustments to them and remembering the team is only as strong as you make it, allows you to maintain control of your bliss.

So where to start? Simple. Open your mouth and talk, honestly—and do it now! Don't wait. Every minute that goes by only puts you that much farther apart. Acknowledge the discontent. Acknowledge the pain. Ask your committed partner what you can do to help. If they are bitter and want you to feel pain along with them, remember, that's a natural, defensive move. Don't be put off by it and whatever you do, don't give up. They are probably testing your commitment and afraid to expose themselves. They're probably thinking, "Oh, they say that now, but they won't follow through." Expect bitterness, but realize, someone has to be the bigger person in order to move forward.

Even if they won't budge, don't give up there. There's so much more that can be done, in either case. Any gesture to show you care and will be supportive will leave its mark. Simple things like telling them, "I love you." or "We are in this together." or "I want to help." or "What can I do?" or "We'll figure this out." confirms to them that you're not abandoning them. It tells them you're not intentionally hurting them. Do something thoughtful or nice for them. Go out of your way to show affection or give them the much-needed backrub or extra time to sleep. Alter your normal behavior to something that you know would give them proof that you are thinking about them and their needs; try to remember all the things they ever wished you'd do, or do more of, and take the time to do it. Put them first. Put you second. Now is not the time to be subtle. Bring out the big guns and put some effort into it. If you don't, things could easily break permanently, beyond repair.

It may take some extra effort, but you will not regret it; quite possibly, it will make you a stronger couple and you can be proud and enjoy the new level of love. I'm not going to sugar coat anything though. Sometimes things are broken too far and both have thrown in the towel. Even if you're afraid you're at this point, you still need to try. Why? You tell me, how content you will be leaving that relationship if you didn't give it your best shot? I'll tell you. You will feel like a failure. Now on the other hand, if you give it all you have (and I mean all you have—no wimpy or lazy stuff allowed here) and your partner won't budge, no matter what, at least you can say you did everything you could. Just make sure you really do.

Remember to ignore your pride and defenses, and really explore how they must feel. Alone. Abandoned. Betrayed. Hurt. Empty. Perplexed. The alienation of your not working together to get through the challenges gives the false impression that you don't care. Every day that goes by without you correcting things leads them to believe you are purposely trying to hurt them or inflict doubt and pain. They analyze what's going on and what you're not doing and are confused as to why you suddenly turned on them. The very person that lifted them so high up and held them when they were flying suddenly let go, and let them drop. They hit the ground hard, and are possibly so broken they can't move, let alone get back up. All they can do is cower on the ground, waiting and hoping that the strength they had, from the union of your lives, will miraculously return. They can't stand up without the reach of your hand. They're not sure they can support themselves for very long without you standing next to them. They may be unable to reach up to you at all, so it will be up to you to scoop them up and support them.

This may sound overly dramatic, but if you've ever been hurt by someone you love, you know I am not exaggerating. Don't think that your partner's hurt feelings are over-played, and for God's sake, don't think they'll just get over it, if you leave them alone long enough! Oh, they may be forced to "get over it" but you will have lost them in the process. Unless that's what you want, get off the brain you're sitting on and do something! It's never too late to let someone know you care. It's never too late to be the bigger person and rise above!

With any change, the choice is up to you. You can be lazy and not explore all of the possibilities. You can sit in your misery and rehash everything that went wrong and ponder that "life is over." You can feel like a big loser in the game of life. But even more easily than you think, you can make positive adjustments to the changes. If you don't feel strong enough or knowledgeable enough to do it on your own, you can seek out learning something new, getting support, or even finding professional help. A positive commitment to yourself, no matter where life takes you, is the key. And then, seriously, nothing can stop you. Nothing.

SH** IS NOT ALWAYS AS IT SEEMS!

Seemingly "bad" things create a greater good.

I bet you'll agree with me that life does not always give you exactly what you wanted? I bet even sometimes, it has dished out the exact opposite on you? Well then, you can relate. Why do things go wrong? Why do things happen to us?

I have to start by reminding you, I'm no expert on anything except having lived over 40 years, at this point in time. Beyond that, it's all my opinion here. In the chapter about not adding to the pile, I ask that people try not to judge other people. Beyond the unnecessary damage you do to the person, I need to point out that unless we are that person and experienced everything exactly as they have, we have no way of knowing exactly what they're all about. We don't know what trials or tragedies they have experienced, or even what they are currently going through. If you were in a tormenting position, would you want someone to judge you and add to your burdens? I can confidently say not. And is it anyone else's business what personal burdens you may be carrying? Again, I can assure you it doesn't help to announce them to the world.

People need to respect others and not use someone's different behavior as an excuse to treat them poorly. Treating someone badly never makes you feel good about yourself. It doesn't matter how much you think they deserve it—it never really makes you feel good, honestly, does it?

So back to my point. Have you ever been misunderstood because someone drew their own conclusion, without knowing all the facts? Bet you have. Well, sometimes life is like that. We draw our own conclusions and assume life is not going our way, when really we don't know all the facts. Sometimes there is a bigger plan, but we have no way of knowing that. Sometimes something that seems "bad" is really something "good" in the long run, not only for you but maybe for other people too.

Sometimes we see the good that comes out of it immediately. Sometimes we see the good come out of it, way down the road. But there are times we can't find the good in it at all. Remember though, sometimes it is there for us to see, but we just miss it. I'll be honest with you. These situations do happen, but sometimes we're not supposed to see the good in it, personally. So don't lose hope.

When life seems to be raining on you, do your best to weather the storm and to help others that may be going through the storm also. Have hope that somewhere, some good did come out of it. You never know. It could be something that changes someone close to someone it happened to. It might be the one thing that put that one person back on their path. It's hard to believe when you can't see everything that's going on. It's hard not to judge when you don't have all the facts. It's hard to know just how that situation or event affects absolutely everyone touched by it.

All I'm asking is, that if you're one of those people that doesn't like to be judged when you're misunderstood, take a breather before being a hypocrite and judging life events. You don't know all of the details. None of us do. But if you think you're one of those brilliant, know-it-alls and can't refrain from assuming things, do us all a favor and assume this: Maybe, just maybe, there's a small chance that you don't know ALL the facts, details, or influences of the situation, event or attitude of others. There is a small chance, you know.

I would also challenge you to prove to me that no one ever benefited somehow by going through a tragedy. You can read story after story of famous, courageous people that went through some personal tragedy before they became an inspiration to the world. Coincidence? I think not. Again, I can tell you personally that after you've gone through something tough in life, only then do you realize how strong or capable you are. You gain courage and faith, and attempt things much less frightening than where you came from. For some of these people, nothing can stop them and they go on to do great things.

My point is, some SH** is there for one purpose…to make you, or someone affected by it stronger. Sometimes it's even more life-changing, where it affects people even more by giving them a whole new perspective; the encounter lifts them up to another plane. If that's the only good you can find in something, isn't that more than enough? So have faith and remember, sometime SH** is there to serve a greater good, whether we can see it, or not.

GRATITUDE ON A GRAND SCALE

 **Why wait for tragedy to appreciate and to help? Help now.**

Gratitude. Why is it so hard to come by? Why does it only seem to appear when there is a loss, and then, only for very short moments? Someone leaves your life. You lose a job. A portion of your health is lost. There is a tragedy with many losses. Suddenly, everyone is grateful for what they once had, or what they still have and did not lose.

I am a firm believer that with every seemingly "bad" thing, a greater good is served. Something bigger, better, and more necessary occurs. I can not always see the direct good that comes about—it is often not for us to see—but I know something positive and wonderful will happen because of it. If we keep our eyes and hearts open to look for the good, most often it will be shown to us.

Here are some examples:

> A. A person leaves a committed relationship and suddenly, the other person realizes how much they took that person for granted and how much they want them back in their life. Why does it

take leaving to clear one's head and admit they should be grateful for this other person? Wouldn't it be easier to show each other how grateful they are to have each other, every day, and avoid the pain, the risk of loss, and the possible end of the relationship?

B. Someone dies. Suddenly, everyone else is grateful it wasn't their parent, or child, or spouse, or close friend, or even themselves. Think of the immense gathering of gratitude for life that exists at every funeral! Most likely, every single person that attends or hears of the loss stops, just for a moment, to appreciate someone in their life. The significant positive thoughts generated from someone's passing away is incredible! It's a "greater good." Sometimes, it even changes how people treat their loved ones for the better…a continuing greater good. The wise will begin to make changes immediately, to express their appreciation to their loved ones, before it's too late.

C. Disease or accident causes a loss of health. Even if complete healing will occur, the loss of your health will remind you very quickly and sharply that we all only have one body to get us through this life. If we don't take care of it, or if it is damaged, it can change your life and cause tremendous pain. Loss of health can easily trigger the loss of other things that you enjoy, and it may be impossible to get some of those things back. Why then, are we so careless with how we take care of ourselves, from what we eat and drink, to lack of exercise and rest, to taking risks that could damage the precious vehicle that carries us through our entire life?

D. A tragedy causes inconceivable losses, often to an extensive amount of people. If you start to consider all the personal and public losses that occur with events to the magnitude of a fire, tornado, hurricane, or terrorist attack, it hurts too much and you try to dismiss it and move on to something less painful. So, where is the good in this, you ask? I can only scratch the surface with how gratitude pours out from anyone that is within the vast broadcast of the tragedy. People are grateful for the time they had with loved ones. People are grateful they, or other loved ones were not taken. People are grateful for the possessions they didn't lose. Again, just scratching the surface. But personally, I feel that the greatest wonder of all appears AFTER the tragedy.

Allow me to digress for a moment to ask you a simple question. If you took a look at all the people of the world and had to consider what the trend is for the majority, as to how they behave during normal, everyday life, how would you honestly answer the following questions? Again, you must consider the majority of the population during a typical day.

1. Do you feel people generally take more than they give? (Consider community service, donations, etc. where they help another person.)

2. Do you feel people are generally more generous, or more selfish and materialistic?

3. Do you feel people are more concerned with themselves, or focus more on serving others?

I know how I would answer, and I'm fairly confident I'd know how you would answer, if you're being completely and brutally honest. Sad, I know, but all too true.

Now, let's go back to the wonder after a tragedy. What happens to people's behavior? An overwhelming flood of human compassion suddenly appears, very often from people that may never have provided assistance of any significance before. The gratitude for what they have in their life compels them provide financial, personal, emotional, and material aid to anyone in need. Some abandon their life routine to provide support, or even risk their life to save or assist someone in need. It is utterly amazing, and not only affects those directly served by it, but anyone that realizes this is going on. An epidemic of heart-filled warmth begins to spread, and it drives many more to consider and even act upon, helping as well. No matter how far away from the site of the tragedy, people around the world suddenly join together to provide any relief they can. Love and compassion and gratitude compels an endless list of generous acts of giving, where there was none, before.

Perhaps the need was not there before, you say? I disagree. The need is always there—it is only more subtle. The world relies on people being grateful, on giving, and on being of service to those in need, to sustain itself. When the world cannot sustain itself (as it does not today), it is merely the results of our failure to serve these needs. My opinion is to not wait for the losses or the tragedies. Let others know what you mean to them, every day, and thank God everyday for what you are grateful for. Prove your gratitude by helping others whenever you possibly can, in any way your possibly can, whether it's just a kind word or gesture, or a selfless act of volunteering or donating. If we each did just a little, the world would turn around. The best part is, you always get more back than what you give, and your heart will be content.

DON'T WATCH OR LISTEN TO SH**

All negativity you're exposed to impacts you, no matter where it's coming from.

In other parts of this book, I explain how what you think about, and especially what you think about a lot, brings it into your life. It's the world's way of knowing what you want, based on that incredible gift of free will that we all have. All I have to do to prove it is to have you think very honestly about things that have happened in your life, and your innermost, deepest beliefs and thoughts before and during it. They don't have to be thoughts that you originated. They can be thoughts that came from anywhere or anyone, written, verbal, or implied. So while you think negativity coming from other places doesn't affect you, that's just not true. If you hear it, read it, or draw any conclusions from anything, it is taking your brainpower. It is consuming your focus, at least at the moment. If you're wise, you'll learn to distance yourself from the negativity, or quickly replace it with a positive thought and release it, so that it doesn't crowd out any of the positive things you wanted to be focusing on.

For this reason, the news, and any negative media like some movies, gossip magazines, soaps, and reality TV that exposes or embarrasses people, are not helpful to you in focusing on the good things you want in your life. Especially if you allow yourself to be absorbed in it and as a means to mock, zone-out, ease your boredom, and waste your time instead of doing something productive. You are giving the negative stuff attention, instead of giving your dreams and positive wishes attention. The negative stuff crowds out the positive stuff and again, just wastes your time and makes it harder to create the kind of life you want. Just like any thought, the more people that give the thought attention, the more powerful it becomes and the more quickly it will come about. It's easy to see why it does not benefit anyone to focus on anything negative, and especially, to go on and on about it, whether on the news or in a person-to-person discussion. Help the world out and change the subject, and your thoughts, to something positive instead.

I'm not saying you can't watch TV or movies, chat online and text your friends, or read as a means to relax, once in a while. I certainly do. Just don't get in the habit of having to do it everyday or throwing yourself in front of the dummy box every time you feel stressed, overwhelmed, tired, or bored. Instead of mindlessly watching TV or chatting or texting night after night, stop the habit and ask yourself, "Is this really helping me, in any way?" Maybe you could get some sleep. Maybe you could work on something around your home. Maybe help someone else. Maybe spend time with someone that would appreciate your time. Read. Learn something. Work on a hobby. Or, just sit and think. Focus on what you want. Do something, anything, more productive that watching stupid stuff on the stupid tube or chatting or texting pointless stuff just to waste time.

Does negativity from the news or even sad or angry songs you listen to make you feel good? No, they don't. Not at all. In fact, even sad songs make you think about the sad and negative feelings, and intrudes on and pushes out the positive things you're trying to focus on. Don't believe me? Again, test it out. Make yourself listen to and read only positive things, and see how much easier it is to focus on what you want and to be more productive at it. You can't say, for instance, that you want to meet that wonderful someone that makes you walk on the clouds and then sit and listen to depressing country songs about jaded relationships. The songs will overpower your positive thoughts of meeting someone special. No matter how much focus you try to give the thoughts of a wonderful person that will love you for exactly who you are, the song is still taking part of your brain and occupying it with a negative thought! Have higher standards for yourself and give yourself a chance! It is so simple to make some simple changes to minimize the negativity that can fly around you, every day.

Pay attention to when and where this happens and make the change. Whether it's a luncheon filled with gossip, the newspaper that seems to only print the awful things that happen, the violent movie, or hours of footage on a tragedy, get away from it! Do what is best for you. Most of us don't need to know every little crappy thing that's going on in the world to function or to do our job, so why immerse yourself in it? So you can feel bad? So you can walk around in gloom all day? Switch to upbeat talk shows, happy radio stations, or volunteer news or something. Stick to the things that you can say will truly benefit you. As always, any little change you make to better your quality of life can make a huge impact on the outlook of your day and what you want in your life. A positive outlook and positive thoughts move you closer to your dreams of living a fulfilled life. Negativity has just the opposite effect. So value yourself enough to make a conscious choice of what is best for you and start making the changes, now!

GET RID OF THE FRIGGEN STRESS OR THAT SH** WILL SNEAK UP ON YOU!

Stress is not your friend. Getting rid of it must be your first priority!

So here I was, nearly finished writing this book, when I realized I didn't talk about stress yet, really. I hadn't addressed the number one irritant most likely to make you get sick, and worse, the most common ingredient to disease. In all my talk about being and living well, I hadn't addressed the worst of our afflictions! It'll make you mentally unwell. It'll make you physically unwell. The combination is literally enough to kill you! That SH** has got to go!

It occurred to me that maybe it hadn't surfaced in all my prolonged thinking, possibly because the topics I cover will automatically relieve the stress, the confusion, the pressure, and the pain. Getting to the root, clearing your head, and taking control of your life can, without exaggeration, cause stress to vanish, instantly. Knowing you are the person you want to be will prevent stress from occurring most of the time. Even then if it does occur, it keeps it from sticking; the SH** just slides off, almost undetected. It can be acknowledged, but then dismissed, quite easily. It's almost like you're standing on a bridge, watching it flow by, far below you. Like you're on a higher level.

Maybe you think I'm on something, and that it's impossible to live without stress. Don't worry, I'm only human too, and when I get lazy or tired or confused, I trip up and let stress in. But I've gotten to the point where I loathe it, and most of the time, I try to think through it quickly, knowing I can dismiss it as soon as I know why it's bothering me. I remind myself that there is always a solution or a better option, and that I'm in control of all of it. I try my best to remind myself of the things I've lectured on in this book. I emphasize these things because it has truly helped me live in a very peaceful and productive state, no matter what is happening around me.

The bulk of my frustration now is in trying to communicate everything I've learned effectively, so that everyone can understand and find the same significance in their life. I know what I've learned, but I'm not sure I can express it in a concise, comprehensive manner to allow others to benefit from it. I am doing my best not to babble in this book, and not to lecture (except where I feel very strongly on something—those topics are very apparent). But mostly, I just want to draw out something you can apply to your life and not bore you in the process! But, I digress; time to get back to the topic.

Stress. It will kill you, if you allow it to fester long enough. There is scientific proof that it causes a magnitude of risk to your well-being, in so many ways. It's no good. That SH** has to go! Please, take a minute right now to think through something that causes you stress. Or take several minutes to think about the various things that are causing you stress. Get to the bottom of each of them as quickly as you can and get rid of them! Again, the experts have written far and wide on this topic, and good friends and family can probably give you some ideas too, so I'm not going to try to teach you how to relieve stress here. If you're really serious about getting rid of it, you'll find as many healthy options and assistance as you can handle.

If you don't want to get rid of it, put on the brakes and stop and think, for the love of sanity! Why on earth would you want to be stressed? To make you feel important? To give you something to complain about? To give you excuses? To punish yourself? Man, that's warped, but in all honesty, it's all too common. I will never understand why people carry stress around without putting any effort into getting rid of it. I don't understand why they don't respect themselves and others more. Then, they're baffled when the SH** sneaks up on them and knocks them down hard, either mentally or physically. They just can't figure it out. Poor souls.

So you get what I'm saying, right? This SH** is probably one of the most critical things you need to face and conquer, right now! Think through what stresses you out, why it stresses you out, and really and truly, WHY it stresses you out. It probably goes back to some pain or fear in your past, or something that's making you feel inadequate. It could be something that you feel is robbing your energy or your time, or frustrating you because you behave differently than you'd really like to.

Whatever the stress, you can find a way to either relieve it or to not allow it to affect you in an undesirable way. But you have to decide you are ready to let it go and put a little effort into changing things, especially if you've neglected it up until now. As always, it's all up to you and what you want for your life. The various topics in this book should get you started, but how far you go is entirely up to you. There really is a higher level out there, and it's so easy to get there, once you get rid of the SH**. Don't let it sneak up on you and swallow you up. It won't sit quiet forever, and it doesn't play nice.

KNOW YOUR PRIORITIES

 **You cannot be happy if you're not living your desired priorities, which show through your actions.**

What are your priorities in life? I challenge you to take one minute and write them down, in order. Just the big stuff, like relationships, work, family, your goals, etc. Okay, now the bigger challenge—prove it! Are these really your priorities or just what you'd like your priorities to be? What are you REALLY putting first in your life? This is what I mean by KNOW your priorities. Be honest with yourself, and then, if what you've been making a priority in your life really isn't what you feel is most important, then you just need to work on changing it. Here's some more thoughts to help you through this process. Try it out! You'll be so much happier!

Test #1: Work
If you list work as your number one priority in your entire life, I have to caution you up front that I rate work as a low priority in my life, so I may be a little biased. Oh, I'm not arguing that work is important to fulfill some of your dreams (such as my dream of writing) and to provide the almighty dollar to live on. I know it's important for that; I'm just one of these people that

don't think it's more important than the people in my life.

I've never been without a job that paid me money—not since I was 16. I have always earned every penny I have, and I do think it's important to have the money to provide for yourself and your children. Being responsible is one thing, but making "having money" more important than the people in your life is dead wrong.

But wait, maybe there is an exception. Maybe you're someone that has no family or relationships and you prefer to be alone. Maybe your work helps people by the million. You wear different shoes than I do, and I respect that. In your case, work probably is and should be, your first priority.

Then there's the rest of us. Those of us that do have relationships with friends, family, and some even have kids. Here's my bias. Personally, all of those people are more of a priority to me than work, meaning I will try my best to never have a job that I give more to than the people in my life. I realize that I work to earn money so that I can provide for and spend time with these people, especially my kids. That is the purpose of my job.

If a promotion or work trip or project threatens to interfere with my ability to be there for something important to my family, I will do my best to avoid it or work around it. If my work threatens to exhaust me so that I have no energy left to play with my kids, I look for a solution. I strive to have a job where I have as many days off as possible, and I take them mainly to spend time with my kids. I especially love scheduling my days off with the days they have off school.

Maybe you don't have that luxury with your job yet, but there's still more you need to think about. Work can produce stress that you carry home with you and throw at your relationships and family. When you do this, you are making work number one in your life. Is that really what you wanted? Just like any bad relationship in your life that you're maybe not supposed to stay in your entire life, your job may be a bad job that you're not supposed to stay in your entire life. Maybe an unfulfilling job is holding you back and causing unnecessary stress on your relationships? Think about it.

Let's be clear here. I'm not giving you an excuse to quit your job before you have a comparable replacement. No, I think you need to be responsible about it. But if you are continuously crabby to the people you love or too exhausted to spend time with them, you need to get out of that job. You're probably not happy there, anyway. Just like a bad relationship, you need to start taking steps towards moving on.

So again, you start by making a commitment to your priorities, and a decision to either make some changes with what's bugging you at work, or start working towards getting another job with comparable pay. Who knows, you might even move up in salary with the change, so why not? Be honest with yourself. Do you like what you do, or would you rather be doing something else? If you're going after a new job, you're in full control. If you have a dream job, start taking steps towards it. If you don't have an ounce of training in your dream job, then settle for doing a job you know to help fund a way to learn your dream job. Maybe you should start reading books about it, from the library.

They're free to use, you know! Maybe you find a mentor to start training you one night a week. Maybe you enroll in a night class towards a degree in your dream work. Maybe you start learning by researching on the internet. It doesn't matter how small the task is, when you start something, you are moving your priorities around.

Try this once, and see how little the annoying things at work bother you now. Once you change your focus and your priorities, the work stress won't stick to you anymore, or at least, less and less often. Don't give up when things get busy. Just know that you are still focusing on a change and stay in control of the stress. Try not to let the SH** that gets flung at you at work stick to you when you leave work. Repel it the best you can while you're earning the money to live the life you really want, and wipe it all off when you leave. The people in your life don't deserve to get it thrown at them when you get home.

Another thing that's helped me is to plant a small symbol or reminder in my work area. As I'm writing this book after my work hours for the job that gives me my bread and butter, I have a small toy that my son gave me sitting on top of my monitor. The toy symbolizes my commitment to go after my dream of writing by writing a children's book about a character my son created one day, while playing with that toy. Anytime work gets long or stressful, I push it all away in my mind, just by looking at that toy. The SH** doesn't stick. I know I won't be doing the job forever, and that each day that passes, I'm closer to living my life the way I want to. Then naturally, I don't worry about irresponsible clients when I want to take some time off to be with my kids. It just won't matter at all in my life within a couple of years. I also changed my passwords to something with the word "writing" in it to remind me every time I log in to my computer that's what my goal is. It really works for me.

Even if you don't want to leave your job, you can plant reminders to get you through everyday stresses. I had a job a long time ago that I absolutely loved. I really enjoyed the clients and all of the coworkers. But the job was so stressful that it almost broke me. Professional as I am, the witch of a boss I had rode me until I had tears of exhaustion on my face. (I could have had her fired for harassment a million times, and in the end, my coworkers almost did.) Anyway, I was really good at my job and she was extremely threatened by it, despite it being an aid in her promotions. She hated that I could accomplish the unbelievable volume of work she'd throw at me with grace and professionalism, and still finish in time to rush home at the end of the work hours to be with my happy family. She hated that I had a family and she was still single, with 10 years on me. She'd constantly set me up for failure and I'd come out with high success. She tried to intimidate me into quitting, but I had no reason but her to quit.

My coworkers went to HR and constantly encouraged and applauded me. I couldn't have survived without them. She was wearing me down though, and I was 8 months pregnant to boot, so I was physically exhausted as well. One day, one of my coworkers brought in a poster of a villain from a popular children's movie. He pointed out that my boss had an unbelievable resemblance to the woman villain, who was horrid in appearance. I screamed out loud with laughter, letting all of the SH** she ever dumped on me release with it. I hung that poster up in my cubicle, right next to my monitor, and just smiled and smiled, especially after she'd just got done screaming at me for no reason again. She couldn't do a thing about it, and my coworkers kept it a secret from her. It kept the SH** from sticking to me, and with HR's help, she finally stopped screaming at me. Eventually, I put the word out I was looking for another job, a client hired me, and I escaped her wrath.

Test #2: You
Do you know where your needs and your dreams are in your priorities? I struggled with this for years, always thinking everybody and everything had to come before me. In some cases, this is true—like your kids—they always need to come first. Now don't go crazy with this thought. I don't mean you need to give them everything they want. Absolutely not! On the contrary, you should only give them what's best for them. What I mean by putting kids first is making sure they have all the love and care they deserve, first and foremost. And yes, this means at your expense. If you have kids, that is your responsibility. But don't get ridiculous here. You need to have a balance.

Balance your work, your relationship with others, going after your goals, and the time with your kids—heavy on the time with your kids, whenever you can. Just like most of us, I had to work to provide a home, clothing, and food for me and my kids; but when I was working, I paid extra to have the kids in good daycare when they were young. I didn't go out with my friends sometimes so I could watch movies and have dinner with my kids, and I let them know I would rather hang out with them. I went without new shoes because my kids needed them. Not so I could buy them the "cool" brand, but so that they had a decent pair. You need to use common sense, here.

Let's get back to you now. Sometimes when life gets busy, we don't take the time to think about what we really want out of life. It's important to take a little time to do this, not just for your sake, but for the sake of the people in your life. I firmly believe that if you're not happy, you can only go so far as to making the people around you happy. So if you love those people, take some time to think about you every once in a while. Think about your goals and dreams and remember, things change as you move through life. So your goals and dreams may change, and hopefully evolve, as you grow older. That's completely realistic and healthy. But you need to identify what those dreams are.

It may be simple or complex, but you need to realize what they are in order to start moving towards them. I think my dream is probably shared by many others, so I'll dip into that. I did not come to this realization over night. It's been years in the making, but it's finally becoming more clear in recent years. Because dreams are a very private thing, I'm not inclined to tell you all of it, but I will share a piece of it with you. Moreover, I haven't figured all of it out, just yet, so I can't put it all together for you yet, anyway. Maybe some day.

As a single mother of three, I worked long hours and felt extremely guilty and tired all the time, just a few years ago. I wasn't giving my kids the time or attention they deserved, so it really aggravated me that work was stealing the time I should be spending with my children. Not only that, I never had time to do anything I wanted to. So, I started to make small changes to move closer to my dream of spending more time with people I cared about and on things for myself.

Slowly, I created ways for this to happen. My first hurdle was realizing that as long as I'm working for a company, I was chained to their schedule. Second, it's a no-brainer that the daily commute to the office stole hours out of my day. All of this time getting ready for and going to work, chained to my desk, and getting back home stole most of my life! Worse, it was keeping me from being there for my kids. I made the decision I'd do what I could to change this.

First off, I made sure my office was close to home and school. Second, my hours or boss had to be a little flexible to allow me guiltless time off. Third, I made sure my associates had a clear picture of acceptable turn-around times. These were the short-term things I could do, but I also set some long-term goals. I realized I wanted to either work from home, eliminating the commute all together, or work in a position that allowed me to set my own hours. Better yet, I wanted to work for myself. Also, I let my kids know that I wasn't working "because that's what everybody does," but because we had to have money to live. I also let them know that if I had a choice, I'd rather spend time with them and that I was working towards that goal. It helped them to understand the rest of what I started to do.

I worked hard and long hours for a short time to prove my worth to the company during a big transition, so that I was recommended for another position when the department was sold. I asked for my kids' understanding and extra help around the house during that time. They hung in there with me, and eventually, the position I was given allowed me to work from home. Now I'm here when they leave, I'm here when they're sick, and I'm here when they get home. I love it and so do they. I'm not taking full credit for making this happen, but I do think the constant, clear picture in my head helped make it happen. Also, I know from experience that God will help those who try to live a good life, ask for help, and believe, and so I am not too proud to ask. I asked my children to pray too, and wah-lah!

Working from home gives me a ton of extra time to stay caught up on household chores and go after other things for myself. My desire to write only grows with time, so over the last 10 years or so, I've been doing little things to work towards this goal. I read a lot on becoming an author. I attend writing classes once in a while. If I see an author coming for a book signing that interests me, I try to stop by. I write in my spare time, which is usually early morning, before the kids get up. And now, as my kids are almost grown and I'll have more time for myself, I'm at a point where I've learned what I need to, to publish my work. I'm glad I took all the little steps here and there, over the last 10 years. I feel like I kind of know what I'm doing!

So I beg you, know your priorities. Be honest with yourself on how your priorities are currently set, and if you don't like it, start making small (or big!) changes to shift those babies around, fast! You will not be happy with your life if you're not living your priorities. It's that simple.

ARE YOU IN A FUNK? ARE YOU IN A RUT? STEP ONE IS TO ADMIT IT!

Pull yourself out of a funk by thinking about what you want and how to get it.

Hey Baby, you're not alone! We all get in a rut, at least every now and then. The good news is, if you admit it, confront it, and ponder it, you can start to think about what you want to change. If you just keep on a-moving, like a mindless robot, your life will feel meaningless and unfulfilling, at least to some degree.

Is it fun, running around like a chicken-with-your-head cut off (by the way, if you have never seen this, they do literally run around—ick!) and then feeling like you didn't get anywhere? To me, this was one of the most defeating feelings. "What's it all for?" I'd ask myself.

So, just go ahead and admit it. There! You just moved forward. Now, in baby steps, if you have to, think about what aggravates you and what you have control over changing, without hurting yourself or others in the process! Maybe you say "yes" too much? Maybe, though, you have no choice in what you do every day, but if you do, do what's best for you and those closest to you.

If you are doing what's best for you and/or those you really care about, then again, admit it! If you are using your time for the most important thing in your life right now, then feel good about it! Just realize that if you don't stay healthy and take care of yourself somewhat, you won't have much energy to take care of others. So do the best you can to take some time to keep yourself healthy and happy, too.

Next, really think through if you could do anything differently, to feel better about it. Have you thought all other options through? Can you get help to alleviate just a little time each day, or at least, each week? If you're feeling overwhelmed and too busy, chances are, it's because there's something else you wish you had time for. Even if it's just time to relax, all by yourself. Which, by the way, is perfectly okay; again, it keeps you healthy and happy, so you have more energy to give to others.

It doesn't matter if you figure out how to have all the extra time you want, right away, but it is important to make an effort towards gaining extra time for yourself or for whatever else you want. For the first month, it might be just thinking about how to modify things to be able to free up the time to do what you really want to be doing. The next month, it might be about starting to get things set up for it.

Here's my example for working moms:

My plan was to get to bed a half-hour earlier and take my vitamins, so I had the energy to get up earlier in the morning. That extra early morning time was all mine to do whatever I wanted, from exercising, to mailing birthday cards, to reading, to getting a jump-start on the housework.

Did I succeed at getting to bed earlier and having that energy right away? Of course not! Life moves quickly. Other people need your help, kids get sick, work needs you to work late; it all happens, despite your new plan. But knowing I was going to get back on track the second my child was healthy, and feeling the blah of that old rut was enough to keep me going. I was thankful that I would have a chance very soon, to try again. That only made me more eager and more dedicated to go after what I wanted.

Once I had taken one baby step, I allowed myself to dream more about what else I really wanted. Now that I knew I had the power to change it, just by thinking up other options, it was more common for me to want to change it. Pretty soon, when I didn't feel content about something in my life, I immediately made myself think about what was bringing me down, and that automatically led me into thinking about what options I had to change it.

Next thing I knew, several years had passed (and my kids grew up to prove it), but I was living my dream, at least, for the most part. Life changes and your ruts change with it, but the key is to control it instead of letting it control you. You have the power to change anything you're not thrilled with. If you don't use that power, the ruts (and life!) will just drag you along.

AREN'T YOU WORTH GIVING MORE TO YOURSELF THAN THE STANDARD CRAP WE SEE THESE DAYS?

Regardless of what others do, don't you want more for yourself?

This is so simple, it'll blow your mind. The most important thing you can do to ensure your happiness is to make sure you behave like the person you want to be. Think about how you, as a hero, would behave. If you wanted to be idolized, respected, and admired, how would you act in the various activities of your day? This applies to everybody and everything, or at least, as much as you can. Pretend there is a video camera on you, constantly, that someone you want to impress can watch at any time, and behave accordingly.

If you're at work, do your work well so that anyone could say you're really good at what you do. I don't care what it is you're doing, and whether it's a job you even like. If you're there, spending all that time there, isn't it worth doing well? Don't you value your time enough to do that? And who really wants somebody scolding you, like a little kid, because you didn't do the job right (this could be your boss, a manager, or even a customer). If you don't want the stress, just do what you should while you're there.

When you're at home, take care of it and of your personal belongings, so that you can be comfortable there and proud to have anyone over. Some say an organized home lends well to an organized life. Now don't go overboard and be anal about it, unless you really want to, but make sure you're content when you're relaxing in your home. Often times, there's more important things going on in life than making sure there isn't a single dust bunny in the house. But it's also nice not to have to clean for a week, just to have someone over. Sometimes spur-of-the-moment invites happen or if you're lucky, you might even have someone drop by. It's nice to not have to be weird because you're embarrassed about how much of a pig you've been.

Regarding your body, the only one you'll ever have, remember that everything that goes in, comes out! Everything you eat or drink has a direct impact on your physical and mental condition. I say mental because certain toxic items (drugs, alcohol, excess sugars, etc.) will affect your mental state, whether it's immediate or long-term. This includes how you feel if you are not content with your body shape or mass. Instead of being a robot where you're just opening the pie hole and dumping in, think about the "hero you" and if you really need or want it.

The same holds true for exercise. What you put in, shows up! Even the smallest amount of exercise helps in so many ways! Long-term, you know the drill, healthy heart, increased energy, longer life, blah, blah, blah. You know this. But let me point out the bigger benefit. You will feel better, mentally. Yes, mentally. Exercise clears your head and makes you feel better in so many ways. There's the body functions, etc., but you also know that you did something to try to stay in shape. A firmer body gives you increased confidence, and this gives you stamina to continue an exercise routine and an incentive to monitor what you consume. You can't lose! Don't make it hard. Make it fun. Even multi-task, if you're a super busy person. How? Oh, there's endless possibilities, like watching your favorite TV shows while you're on a stationery machine or lifting weights, pulling the kids in a wagon while you go for a walk, hiking with a friend you wanted to catch up with, or my favorite, reading or jotting down notes or to-do's for my day while I'm on the elliptical machine. Just take a couple of things you want to accomplish and put them together with exercise—I know you can come up with something!

Then there's what you do with your time, and what you do with your life. Do you feel like you spend time each week doing something that has purpose for you and is fulfilling to you? Do you value your time? You should. If you don't, you will feel like a hamster running on his wheel, in his cage, because your life is equivalent. You just don't go anywhere unless you put some meaning in to what you're doing. If you're not doing this now, the change does not have to be dramatic. It can be the difference of just taking an hour a week, to start, to do something that you've always wanted to, or to make you feel great about yourself. Maybe it's helping someone in your family, or volunteering. Maybe it's spending time with an old friend. Maybe it's working on your home or a hobby. Maybe it's researching something you've always dreamed of trying. Anything that is important to you. You can't spend all your time doing unfulfilling things or you will be very, very unhappy.

Speaking of your time, do you ever stop to look at who you spend your time with? Are they draining your time or are they worth hanging out with? Do they appreciate you? Do they have a positive, nurturing impact on you and others? Do they help you use your brain, or force you to turn it off? Are they good for you? If not, stop wasting all that time with them and use it in a better way. It's impossible for people of different values and influences to not rub off on each other, eventually. If they are tossing negative SH** or risks at you or anyone around you, why do you hang out with them? Again, you are cheating the world and the people that do care about you. You can find a million ways to very politely distance yourself and cease seeing these types of people, if you value yourself enough. Sometimes you just have to tell people, "Hey, that's not cool."

As long as you value yourself and want more for yourself that the standard crap we see these days, you can figure out a way to change things and to evolve into what you really want. You are on this earth for a darn good reason. You are highly valued by your Creator. Don't you think you could try a little to make yourself realize how precious you are? Shouldn't you be better to yourself? What's the point in being here, anyway, if you aren't living your life the way you want to? There's no better time to start.

YOUR LIFE DOESN'T HAVE TO BE THE NORMAL SH**

Your life can only be as good as you believe. Maybe your beliefs need some work.

Everybody probably knows that positive thinking is the way to go. Naturally, it makes you feel better, gives you hope, and brings more positive things to you. Most people try this on for size at some point in their life, but then quickly discard it, thinking they're only fooling themselves. I learned in my early 40's (yes, it took me that long!) that there's more to it, and it has indeed changed my life. Actually, I can brag and give you proof that I changed my life. Let me explain.

The older and wiser I become, the more I know there is just so much to learn. I happen to enjoy reading and listening to books on CD as one way to explore something totally new. A good friend recommend a book that opened my eyes, my heart, and my life (Thanks, Lisa!). I strongly recommend it. The title is, <u>The Secret</u>, by Rhonda Byrne

I've come to the realization that your most prominent thoughts become your life. What you think actually becomes your life. Your mind actually tells the universe what you want your life to be like. I have listened to books on CD several times already, in an effort to retrain my natural way of thinking, so it's not something I can even attempt to sum up for you here. It takes some time and effort to retrain the brain! But I can give you a taste of my personal experiences.

My whole point in bringing this up to you is that I discovered that my life didn't have to be the "normal SH**" everyone perceives as the life of a middle-class single mother of three. Actually, no, let me correct that. I realized my life didn't need to be the "normal SH**" that I perceived as what my life should be. It was all me, creating the life I was leading, based on my thoughts of what I thought had to be there, based on my status. Exposing myself now, I'm going to start with my negative thoughts on what I thought my life had to be:

A. As a divorcee with kids, no one worthwhile would want to date me, until my kids were grown.

B. As a single mother of three, I'd always be overwhelmed with the kids' needs and schedules, and usually running late and behind on everything.

C. As a single mother of three, I'd struggle financially and would always have to work hard to be able to barely pay the mortgage.

D. Until the kids were grown, I'd never have time for anything I wanted to do for myself. I would always come last and never look my best because I couldn't invest the time or money.

E. Now that I'm over 40, my body would start to show signs of aging (weight gain, wrinkles, not as fit).

Now I know that most mothers out there can easily relate to this, but whoever you are, I want you to take a minute now, and make a list of what you think your life has to be. Be honest with yourself. List out what you are really thinking, most of the time. What do you perceive as your life, and how it "has to be?" Trust me, this exercise is worth the couple of minutes I'm asking you to take!

At the time I'm writing this section in 2007, just a couple of weeks after I read that first book on this topic, I'm starting to realize the power of my thoughts and trying to focus on what I really want, not on what I think it has to be like. I've already seen changes in the areas I've changed my thoughts on. It only takes as long as you decide, based on your passion on that particular thing. So have you made your list yet? Please stop and do so. If nothing else, it makes you aware of what you're thinking! Make your list and then come back to me, and then, let's continue the process.

Okay, now that you've made a list of what you think your life is like, let's continue on. I need to use my previous list as an example to make my point. My list is my honest inside opinion on my life—NOT what I really want, but it's controlling my life. In all cases, they are exactly where I'm at in life:

A. "As a divorcee with kids, no one worthwhile would want to date me, until my kids were grown."

I can't seem to meet the right guys. My friends and family have told me they're baffled, because they think I'm a premium catch. Sorry to sound conceited, because I'm not, but I can't argue with what they tell me. I'm physically attractive and fun, successful and honest, caring and intelligent. Really, no big flaws, especially if you compare me to the rest of the single people out there! Still, my thoughts are, "As a divorcee with kids, no one worthwhile would want to date me, until my kids were grown." So guess what, I'm single more than I'm dating. I struggle to find good guys to date, and have pretty much given up, for now. Now that I realize what I'm doing to my life with these negative, ridiculous thoughts, I'm working on changing my thoughts to, "I'm a really decent person and could really make a deserving person happy. I'd like to have a good man in my life." I wasn't expecting to be dating for like, another 5 years, so I'm still adjusting to this one!

<u>PROOF IT WORKS:</u> It seemed like an invisible, loser-repelling wall was suddenly constructed around me. Guys in the bars pretty much quit hitting on me, or would leave me alone, after just a few words. I suddenly started having quality conversations with people I met, while I was out, and if some guy that was trouble expressed an interest in me, someone always knew him and would ward him off before he even got to talk to me. I suddenly had everyone looking out for me, and I didn't loathe going out to the bars, worried that some drunk guy was gonna try grinding me on the dance floor anymore. They were just staying away. It's much more enjoyable now, and kind of cool!

B. "As a single mother of three, I'd always be overwhelmed with the kids' needs and schedules, and usually running late and behind on everything."

My head was always spinning with a flurry of things to remember and do that day, from the second I woke up in the morning, until it hit the pillow, completely exhausted that night. This was easy to see, it was coming from my thoughts of, "As a single mother of three, I'd always be overwhelmed with the kids' needs and schedules, and usually running late and behind on everything." I hated this the most, so I changed my thoughts immediately to, "I have relaxing days, with ample time to get every where we need to be, on time, every time."

PROOF IT WORKS: I've been able to get to everything, including my hobbies and more time with family, friends, and vacations! I am relaxed during the day, my house is in better order, and I rarely feel overwhelmed. My head is clearer, and I'm more content. It feels SO good!

C. "As a single mother of three, I'd struggle financially and would always have to work hard to be able to barely pay the mortgage."

I'm always wondering how I can pay the next bill. Even though I make a good salary in my non-writing job, I end up having to use credit cards and take a second mortgage to get through, month-to-month. I can blame this on my thought of, "As a single mother of three, I'd struggle financially." New thought, that I try to plug into my head every day, "I will make $2 million dollars by this time next year and be in a position to help a large volume of needy children and never worry about my bills again. In the meantime, I will always have more than enough to make ends meet." This may seem extreme to you, but you'll get it, if you read the book!

PROOF IT WORKS: Somehow, in the last week or so, I've got enough money to go around, and I haven't done anything different. Things are just falling that way. I don't have my $2 million dollars just yet, but I'm also not entirely believing it yet. Some day I will, and it will fall in my lap, I'm sure.

D. **"Until the kids were grown, I'd never have time for anything I wanted to do for myself. I would always come last and never look my best because I couldn't invest the time or money."**

Without even knowing it, I started to change my way of thinking about taking time for myself. Through some other things I've read or listened to, I explored more creative ideas on how to make some time for myself, and value my contentment as a natural way to be the best mom I could be. I started whittling away at these types of thoughts. So slowly, I have found more time for myself. That makes me a more energetic, happy mom, so it's all good. I continue to refine this thinking into, "I put myself first whenever I can, because when I'm content, I can be the most positive influence on those around me, especially, and most importantly, my kids."

PROOF IT WORKS: Lately, I seem to have more time to get to what I want to do, especially staying caught up on sleep! I have more confidence and often talk to people I don't even know, especially if I think I can make their day better. Why did I wait so long?

E. "Now that I'm over 40, my body would start to show signs of aging (weight gain, wrinkles, not as fit)."

Continuing on with the last couple of thoughts, in the last year or so, being over 40 seems to really have taken root. All that nasty stuff that people say happens, started happening. I know where I went wrong! After turning 41, I wondered, where is all this bad stuff that happens around 40? It's gonna hit me soon! I don't want it to! My bad thoughts of, "Now that I'm over 40, my body would start to show signs of aging (weight gain, wrinkles, aches and pains)" wrecked my life, again! I was fine, up until 41ish because I didn't believe it all, and truly, didn't think about it before then. I had told myself before that it wouldn't happen to me. I was too health-conscious. But then I let it creep in my thoughts, and it took over my body! Just like that! All of a sudden, I had wrinkly eyes! My skin was starting to sag, and not to be gross, but the spare tire I never, ever had inflated, out of nowhere! Well, I tried reading up on the latest trends in dieting and fitness. I refuse to try anything outside of normal healthy eating, so I didn't jump on the bandwagon, but I did everything I should to control my weight. Still, here it came! So as soon as I read about this, I changed my thinking to, "I DO have the body of a 20-some year-old! Firm skin, flat belly, and youthful face."

<u>PROOF IT WORKS:</u> After struggling with the spare tire for about a year, I have a sexy, flat belly again. I didn't do ANYTHING different. As a matter of fact, I haven't had as much time to exercise lately, but I've had periods like that before. I never had results like this. I also quit worrying about eating that "extra something" here and there. I decided I'm always going to have a firm, healthy, strong body, and that's all there is to it. People have noticed, too. My clothes fit better and I feel sexy again.

Now your life should not be all gloom and doom, unless that's where your thoughts are. I also had some positive thoughts about what I wanted in life. I thought about these all the time. And guess what? I have all these things, and have for the last few years. The key here again was that I thought about and dreamed about these things, all the time. They were a main focus. Now, you're going to want to argue that I made some of these things happen. Well maybe, some of them, a little; that comes naturally when you think about it all the time. But some of it just happened to me. Here's my positive thought list, of which, I have all!

- I want tons of family and friends. I have hundreds of both, and most are solid, do-anything-for-you people. I am truly blessed.

- I always wanted to work from home and spend as much time as possible with my kids. An out-of-state company buy-out set me up nicely several years back. While three of the staff were involved, I'm the only one left with a job. Moreover, they counted my years of previous employment towards my vacation time. I have the maximum days off that the company gives. I don't have a problem getting a day off, whenever I want it.

- I wanted a home in the country with a huge yard, lots of flowers, and a garden. I sold the tiny house in town, that I bought with the divorce settlement and made a $60,000 profit and had just enough to buy the house I stumbled on, by accident. The country house had been on the market for over a year, just waiting for me to discover it.

- I wanted an SUV to haul around my kids and their friends. Got in a car accident that totaled my car. I decided then and there I needed something safer to drive and had to buy it.

See what I mean? Focus on what you want. Put the thought in your head and watch it come to you!

Well, thanks for helping me with my therapy. I really do appreciate it. Now it's your turn. Take that list you made, and start with one or two that really, really bug you, but make sure you touch on all of them, very soon. Write down what you want and how you want your life to be. It must be a positive thought. So instead of writing, "I don't want to worry about money anymore," write, "I have more than enough money for everything I want."

Now, if you are serious about changing your life, put the effort into reading or learning more about specific ways to change your thinking. It can really whip you through the whole process so you can begin making changes immediately. If you really want changes in your life, please put some real effort into exploring this whole concept more. You'll only thank me and everyone else encouraging you!

Briefly, there's three basic steps to change these things in your life:

1. Think about it, all the time. Focus on it, in a positive way, as often as possible. Remove any negative thoughts and discussions, including your thinking about the past, if it's not positive! If outside media or people expose you to negative thoughts on the topic, try to minimize it or eliminate it. The more passionate you are about visualizing what you really want, the faster you will have it.

2. Believe, believe, believe. Don't worry about how, when, or why, just believe. It will come to you, if you believe. It must be your true, deep-down belief. It must be your bare feelings, as they always win. If you have beliefs etched in that you'd like to change, change them! You control all of it. Begin by picking apart why you feel that way and get to the bottom of it. Analyze whether it really helps you or not, and if not, dismiss it and replace it with your new belief. It really is that easy. Educate yourself on the desired belief so that you can accept it without any doubt. Talk to family and friends, research it on the internet or at the library, join a support group or chat room; just do whatever it takes!

3. Even before you receive it, be grateful for it. Thank God or the universe or the spirit (take your pick) for it, often and whole-heartedly. Keep focusing on having that positive thing in your life. Genuine, constant appreciation brings you more of it and brings it to you faster.

Easy, isn't it? The hardest part for me is changing how I think, and changing my actions accordingly. That's why I listen to that book that my friend recommended on CD often, and grab other books on the topic to learn what I can from them. I want it to come naturally to me, continuously. I've been so happy with the little changes I've seen in less than two weeks with just dipping my big toe in, I can't wait to see what's ahead, once I jump in. I keep working on changing my thoughts more and more, every day. It's coming along nicely.

Now once you've read the book, you'll probably interpret things in your own way. For me, it's so simple, I wish someone would've hit me aside the head with it 30 years ago. It's everything I learned growing up. It's just that at that time, I didn't translate it this far. I've been taught since I was little that everyone has the right to "choose." Everyone is born with "free will." I thought this meant that everyone has the ability to decide for themselves each time they made a decision, to choose good or bad. Easy enough.

But after reading the book, I know it goes much deeper than that. Now I think having the right to "choose" and to have "free will" means that we each get to decide what we want and how we want our life to be. Yes, it's about making choices, but it's more than that. Through what we think about, we are asking to have that particular thing in our life. It doesn't matter whether it's good or bad, if you think about it, you're asking for it!

This makes sense to me. As a Christian, I believe in praying as a way of asking God for what I want in my life. I pray mostly through the thoughts in my head. I have always believed that those things I ask for (think about) the most are the prayers that will most likely be answered. So you see, what I think about the most shows up in my life. You can think of it as praying, as visualizing, or as summoning the universe and nature. It doesn't matter—it's all the Being. I know God created it all and makes it all available to each and every one of us. It's our own shortcomings that keep us from receiving it.

Now again, without getting into the beautiful details you'll find in the book, I need to remind you that there's no distinction between good and bad, positive or negative thoughts. This process doesn't know the difference between you saying, "I want…." and "I don't want…." It just goes after whatever you're thinking about. So do you see how damaging negative thoughts, complaints, gossip, and pre-conceived bad thoughts can be? They can ruin your life! Stop the negative thoughts immediately and see how much happier you are! If someone around you is being negative, try to avoid them or politely let them know you don't want any part of it. Hearing, watching, or reading negative things causes you to think about it, and thus, taints what you're really wanting to focus on.

Turn your desires into positive thoughts and focus on them. The more often and the deeper you believe, the faster it will appear in your life. As the book instructs you, don't worry about how, just imagine you have it already and be grateful for it, and it will come to you. If you really want to see some major changes in your life, pick it up and retrain your brain. You won't regret it!

POSTSCRIPT: This chapter was written in 2007, just after I read that recommended book. That book led me to a couple other books, that helped me change some of the thoughts I had inherited throughout my life. With a clear picture of how God meant things to be (at least, being more aware of one small sliver of His gifts to us), I immediately went to work on changing my thinking and removing the negative things in my life. I dug down to my heart's desires, feelings, and habitual behaviors and changed the ones that were not allowing my dreams to evolve, and I started having perfect days, whenever I made myself focus. My mind is most clear while I'm lying in bed, either at night or in the morning, or when I'm outside walking. I took the time to visualize what I wanted and I was grateful, just knowing it was mine because I asked for it. It made me feel elated, every time. Within 6 months, I had changed my life in the most needed areas. I was suddenly with the man of my dreams. I was able to refinance back to one mortgage, and my money worries were no more. I had more time with my family and friends. I found new ways to take care of myself, physically, including healing some very old injuries. I was pursing my dreams and doing things I had always wanted to try. I continue to work on all of this, but most of my days feel perfect. I don't exaggerate. When I focus, I have perfect days. I know now, heaven can be in the present, living these perfect days. It's not just there for after we die.

GOOD AND EVIL DOES EXIST

Every part of your being is occupied with one or the other; there is no empty space. Crowd out the evil with the good.

Okay, don't pull away now, thinking I'm trying to preach to you. I'm not, and even if you felt that way, remember that what you believe is still completely your choice. I'm not a "bible-thumper" but I've been through enough in life to tell you that I know the forces of good and evil play a strong part in each an every life on this planet, but more importantly, in the level of happiness you can achieve in life.

There are many beliefs out there, but as far as I know, they all come down to this, in the very simplest form. I myself, do believe in God, and do believe both forces are there because God gave us free will and He lets us choose everything. Did you hear that? YOU CHOOSE EVERYTHING. Again, please stay with me because I think you'll want to know about this, if you don't already. I'm guessing you really do already know, but it never hurts look at another perspective.

Let's start with the heart. Not the physical heart, but the soulful side of the heart. I believe how you feel about yourself is directly related to how much good is in your heart. I believe that the areas of your heart that do not contain good are free game for evil. The more good that's in your heart, the less chance evil has to get in. The less good that's in your heart, the more room there is for evil to set in. Make sense, so far? Lucky for you, good is always the more powerful of the two. The benefits of choosing good will always make you feel better and last longer than if you choose evil. So here's how it works, very simply.

Whenever you choose good, or do something good, it fills your heart with good. Some of the very, very few examples include:

- Being kind
- Being patient
- Helping someone, without expecting something in return
- Smiling
- Being fair
- Controlling your temper
- Being honest
- Being grateful
- Appreciating nature
- Being respectful
- Using your extra time to better yourself
- Taking care of your health (adequate sleep, exercise, eating/drinking habits)
- Giving to the needy
- Praying
- Attending a church service
- Sharing (physically, mentally, emotionally…any little gesture helps)
- Not starting or spreading negative rumors, even if you think the person deserves it (If you can't say something nice, say nothing at all)

The more you do, the more full of good your heart will be. Again, it is this simple! Now, where your heart does not contain good, there is room for evil to creep in. The less full your heart is, the more chance evil has. The more full your heart is, the less chance evil has, and in fact, it rarely wastes its time on a fairly full heart. It would rather spend its energies on an empty heart.

Evil is very simple, too. The more that it occupies your heart, the less chance that you'll be good to yourself or to others. And that's all evil looks to do—to make you miserable and to make others miserable. Don't be misled by the short-term effects that appear to be benefits of doing something you know isn't right. In the end, it will make you feel bad. Think about it. Evil isn't there to make things good for you, and bad for others; it makes it bad for you too. Evil is all about misleading and lying, and you need to realize this when you're in a position where you actually think that doing something wrong is okay, it's lying to you. You know deep down that later on, it's not going to make you feel good. Evil DOES NOT want you to feel good, but it may mislead you by dangling a temporary, "this will make you feel good" lie in front of you. In the long haul, you will not feel good, and it will require that much more good to take back the ground you just lost.

Once you let evil set in, you need to push it out again, by doing good. Oh, but don't fret. Remember, good is the stronger of the two, so it doesn't take much to shove it out. All you have to do is choose. Each time you choose good, it gives a strong kick to any evil that's hovering. Before long, it will take off and go look for an emptier heart to mess with.

Trust me on this one, and look around. Make your own observations with other people you've crossed paths with. The selfish, greedy people. Do you really think they're happy when they look in the mirror? One really easy way to tell how they feel about themselves is by watching how they treat other people. If they're genuinely kind and giving, they are probably happy. If they are mean or temperamental, they are probably miserable. Oh, one important thing. A miserable person doesn't always mean the evil in their heart is outweighing the good. It could also be that they're very close to someone in that situation, where all of the bad is being poured over them, as well. You never know what people have been through, or what they're dealing with. Remember, you can't go wrong by being good to everyone you meet. It feels good to rise above, no matter how crappy someone is to you.

Your mind is very closely linked to all of this. Doing good is tied to good thoughts. Good thoughts keep your mind open and clear, and give the mind room to flourish. It brings peace and allows you to do more good, which has a positive effect on others, and therefore, on the world! Yes, one person does make a difference. The good that you do contributes to the good in the world, as a whole. Again, the more good in the world, the less room for evil. It really is all quite simple.

Anyway, back to the mind. Once again, the more good that's present here, the less room there is for evil. And when it comes to the mind, it gets very tricky. Evil likes to creep in here very quietly. First, it tries to weaken you. This takes many forms, from bad things that happen to you or to people around you, to fatigue, to simple temptations. Unless you have the strength that the presence of good creates, evil has a good chance of getting into your head and taking hold, at some point.

Evil goes right for your weak spots, whatever they may be. There's no playing fair. It will create self-doubt, remove your self-esteem, and lead your mind into chaos. It will lead you to wrong choices and try to throw you into a hole so deep that you are constantly preoccupied with worry on how to get out of the hole. Once you're preoccupied with all that worry and shame, you don't have any time to stop and think about what's best for you or for others. Your mind is constantly spinning, and rarely focuses on anything. You become confused over simple decisions, and are easily led to making the wrong choice.

Usually, this doesn't happen overnight. Usually, evil will peck away at your for years. It makes good use of any hurt, bad memories, and shame from the past and presents you with a terrible lie. It tells you, you don't deserve a good life. It tells you, you don't deserve to be happy. So I ask you, is evil honest, or completely lying to you? I think you know. Evil is lying to you, because if you knew the truth, you would be in a position to make yourself happy, and then to also help others be happy. That is the last thing evil wants.

Now don't feel bad if this has happened to you, or if this is the state you feel you are in right now. The good news again, is that good is much stronger than evil. Once you realize how badly evil's been messing with your head, and your life, you can start to make changes to have the life you deserve. The life that each and every one of us deserves. No one has been given preference; we all deserve to be happy.

Every step in the good direction weakens the evil. When it comes to the mind, it may take some re-training. Don't give up. Every good choice you make is a bad one you passed over, and every little bit helps! Please realize that good choices are there for you to make, constantly, and that every choice has an effect on something else. Good brings good. Bad brings bad. See? It's so easy.

So let's say you realize that evil has embedded a few lies in your brain, or even in someone close to you, and you'd like to flush them out. You can do something immediately. Acknowledge that you're on to this vicious plan. You know, or at least suspect, these are lies and you want to get rid of them. One of the very first things you should do, if you have any spiritual beliefs, is to pray. Ask God to help make you strong so that you can overcome the lies that have been planted. Every serious, faithful prayer you put in is another block of good that you're collecting, and again, the more good, the less evil. I can't explain how powerful prayer is; it's something you need to experience for yourself. They say, "Faith can move mountains." I know, from my own experience, that faith and prayer can make changes more powerful than moving a mountain. Try it, and you'll see. But you have to have faith and you have to believe. Again, it's your choice.

More good news. People have gone through this, since man first existed on this earth, and some of the goodness has spilled over into them wanting to help others. If you want to help yourself, realize there are a ton of books with extremely helpful ideas in them. Get to a library or a bookstore and find a book on overcoming your particular battle. Go online to find support groups, and if you feel so inclined, meet with a counselor or psychologist. Many company employee assistance programs and health insurance plans offer this to you at little or no charge and everything's confidential. Personally, I think each and every one of us could use a good talk, every now and then. I guarantee there's help out there, somewhere. Every effort you make will do nothing but help you get to that fulfilled life that we all deserve. Don't let the lies that may have been started as far back as your childhood fool you. Don't let evil control your life. How you live your life is your choice.

Your choice may lead you to want to learn more about something, or get more ideas on how to improve yourself. Again, people have written book after book on just about anything out there! I really enjoy browsing through the library, and have checked out countless "self-improvement" books, just to get ideas on different things. I found a lot of ideas I liked and have applied them to my life. I was also pleasantly surprised, as it's helped me to understand other people too, especially those I couldn't see eye-to-eye with. Different people have different things that work for them, and sometimes, different views as well. That's why I like the library so much. You can take away what you like from a book and apply it, and leave what doesn't work for you, and then turn around and get a different one. All this, and I haven't spent a dime. I figure, if I learned anything from it, it was worth my time. The mind is an incredible thing, and it has an infinite ability to learn and absorb and recreate itself.

Empty space allows room for evil to creep in. If you're not using your mind for positive things and positive thoughts, you're allowing room for the evil lies, ideas, and chaos to creep in. I lecture you on this in many other places in this book, so please check it out. Please stay focused on what you want your life to be and how you want to be. Don't get me wrong, I don't think you need to constantly occupy yourself with something. When it's time to relax, relax, but don't be lazy too often. Sitting around vegging all the time only allows more time for evil tricks of the mind. On the other hand, if you're using your mind for something positive, you're controlling that space; there's no room for the evil to play.

And through all this, please remember, if you feel weak or tired or defeated at times, don't worry. If you feel incapable of making any strides at the moment, just close your eyes and pray for strength. It will come, if you choose it. Rest, if you need it, but ask for strength, as you close your eyes. Every baby step you make towards good and flushing out the lies will only help push the evil out. Soon, you will feel strong again and find peace, more and more often, until it is constant in your life. Don't let the setbacks scare you. Remember, setbacks are all part of the evil plan but can always help us learn, and in the end, good will always conquer.

ARE YOU FOLLOWING YOUR DREAM? WHY NOT?

Dreams are meant to come true now. Why are you not allowing it?

Do you ever think about something else that you would rather be doing? Got something you've always wanted to try? Just because you don't know how, don't let it stop you. Don't let your mind get clogged with what's standard for everybody else. Rise above the boring SH**. Give yourself a lift! We all owe it to ourselves to go after new things, so why not start now?

The sad truth is, a lot of us don't go after our dream because we're afraid we'll fail, and then we won't have any dreams anymore. Does that apply to you? Is the fear of the unknown or the fear of failure holding you back? Think about it a second. Does this make sense to you? Would you advise someone close to you to NOT pursue their dreams because they might not make it? I really hope not. Then why would you advise yourself not to pursue your dreams?

Okay, maybe you're past that, but you've got other obstacles. Most of us do. Wait, maybe obstacles isn't always the best word choice. There may be actual obstacles, but there also may be other good reasons, like raising your kids, for instance. Kids are NOT obstacles. They are a privilege to have in your life and they have to come first. But all the obstacles and reasons in the world can't keep you from going after something you really, really want. So again, if you're not moving in the direction of your dream, be honest with yourself as to why. Once you've tackled that, there's no stopping you!

Ideally, our dreams are meant to come true when we're prepared to embrace them and appreciate them. We don't always know the timing, and sometimes we get frustrated when we make a move towards it, and it doesn't happen. Please remember that we don't always know what's best for us; we don't always know where we're supposed to be, down the road. Sometimes, we have to accept that our best efforts will get us closer to life fulfillment, even if we don't understand the roadblocks, detours, and complete changes of direction along the way.

That said, what are you doing to get started on your dreams? If your response is, "Nothing, right now." Shame on you! Do something! Again, big, small, or medium-sized, it doesn't matter. Any attempt you make moves your forward. If you're like me, you'll feel more confident doing your homework first. Yes, there usually is homework, if it's something new to you.

It's easy though. First, make sure you know what it is you want. You can't chase it down if you don't even know what you're looking for. Second, think about the steps you need to go through to get there. You probably don't know the steps, so this is where the homework starts, but it's easy, fun homework! There's always a way to get started. You will find the more you immerse yourself in it, the faster that wish will become reality. Here are some ideas on how to start:

1. Talk to people that might know about it or that are already doing it. Experts in the field are invaluable!

2. Seek out everything there is about it on the internet, not just on the direct topic, but associations or chat rooms related to it. Join them, if desired!

3. Research everything about it at the library (You do know library cards are free and you can request just about anything in print or on a recording, right? Free videos, magazines, software, the whole gamut!)

4. Look for classes, seminars, and just anything related to it.

Maybe you have a very busy life and only have one hour a month to dedicate to this. So? Isn't one hour better than no hours? Even if you're limited on time, realize it doesn't have to consume a lot of your time. Just start in, a little at a time, and before you know it, you'll be doing it. That's how I started writing. Very slowly and quite often, with a lot of time in between. It's your dream, so it'll probably hook you pretty fast. Also, you'll suddenly find yourself tuning in to other things around you that may be related to it. One thing leads to another, and another, and another. You'll be amazed how things just start opening up, when you open yourself up to it!

Again, if it doesn't move quickly right away, be patient. I first started looking into writing as a career back in

1998, when a self-paced course caught my eye. That self-paced, one-year course took me 8 years to complete, but dammit, I completed it! No, I wasn't lazy. Keeping my life and my kids' lives in balance is my first priority. Occasionally, I would feel guilty about not getting back to my course work (especially when a year would go by with no action) but I trusted that the timing was all as it should be.

In case you're wondering why it took me so long, I'll explain. See, I had been doing SOMETHING over those 8 years, and it's not super, out-of-the-ordinary. With three small kids, I separated from my husband and soon after, we were divorced. I moved to an apartment, then a starter home, and finally my current home. I always worked around 50 hours a week. I went through two car accidents with my kids, the last one leaving me with a broken neck. If you think about how any one of these events can consume your life as you just try to survive, you understand how the 8 years just flew by. You could call them "set-backs," but in reality, it's just living life. We all have something, but we all must realize that and never give up. By the way, I survived the broken neck just fine!

The more I realized that writing would help me succeed in so many other goals (working for myself, having time to spend with my family when they need it, helping others on a large scale, feeling fulfilled in my work) the more I naturally focused more and more free time towards this goal. Before I knew it, I wasn't dreaming about it any more, wondering, "What if?" No, I was DOING IT! And boy, does it feel good!

Maybe I had to go through those things to give me the confidence I needed to be a writer. For me, I have to have a clear, open mind to write quality stuff, and I think life helped me get there. Looking back, I realize they were not "obstacles," but directionals. My kids are nearly grown and pretty independent now, so I have a clear conscience when I sit down for hours and write. Work has slowed down, so I'm not exhausted at the end of the day (most days). I'm pretty sure that after all I've been through, I can do anything I set out to do, so I'm not afraid of failure anymore. But sweeter than anything, all of these years helped me realize the type of writing I wanted to do so that I could put my whole heart into it and make it worth reading. You can't tell me somebody up there doesn't know what He's doing. Sometimes we just need to keep the faith.

So get rid of the excuses and start laying some groundwork to get to where you want to be. Then, be ready and appreciative when it's time for your dream to commence. Don't you think your life should be spent doing things you enjoy? I'm a firm believer that we're drawn to do what we enjoy, and what we're good at, as our ultimate destiny. But you have to pay attention and take the steps towards that. If you don't, I don't believe you can ever feel completely fulfilled in life. No one else can take your steps for you. You have to do it for yourself. So go for it, and have fun!

WHAT IS YOUR SELF IMAGE?

Knowing how you see yourself helps you understand what you do and how to change, if you want to.

Who do you think you are? Really. I'm asking you. How do you see yourself—what is your self-image? You probably don't realize what a tremendous impact your self-image has on your satisfaction in life, how you behave, and what you portray to others. Your self-image can help you to succeed or fail at anything you do. Let's take a closer look.

If you were to describe your inner-most self, in the form of a person, what would it be? Now be honest with yourself; this is just for you. No one else has to know. Do NOT describe an impressive image of what you think people expect you to be. Describe yourself at the age level and attitude that your heart REALLY feels, most of the time. We may see ourselves differently at different times, but go with how you view yourself, deep, deep down, the majority of the time. Here are some common examples:

   A. A playful child, that doesn't want to grow up
   B. An overweight or unappealing child, that everyone teases
   C. A rebellious teenager

D. An adventure-seeking teenager
E. A struggling, stressed-out parent with little control
F. An authoritative parent that controls all in your household
G. Yourself, at a certain decade of your life (teens, twenties, thirties, etc., regardless of your current age)
H. An unattractive, plain, boring person waiting for someone to understand you
I. An attractive, sexual person, pretending to be overly confident
J. A sad victim of the world or of another in a relationship, with no control
K. A professional, chasing the almighty dollar and the power that comes with it
L. A giver, seeking to help people in any way you can
M. A point-out-the-flaws-in-others person, because you think it makes you look better to others
N. An achiever, yearning to learn and grow and to experience a more wonderful life
O. Someone else you've encountered, at a certain time of their life (it's very common to imitate a parent or authority figure from the past, as you find yourself in those situations)
P. An aging, out-of-shape person, struggling to hide your discomfort with it

Does this help you get your image going? Your image may be a combination of some of these things, or not on my example list at all. Also, no matter your age, your self-image can be any age. No matter your status or situation in life, your self-image can be anything at all. Now I've mixed physical images with emotional images here. You have both, so to really help yourself here; you need to understand what your physical image is of yourself, along with your emotional image. Can you describe yourself to yourself now? If you need more time, put this down for a while and really take the time to get to the core of who you think you are. This honesty can change your life.

Okay, now on to the meat of why, first of all. Why do you have this image of yourself? Is it because that's who you were told to be, or what society or adults in your past told you to be? Was it something someone else said or did in the past? Is it because you suddenly found yourself in a new situation and decided you didn't know how to act, so you naturally imitated someone else you observed in that role? What made this self-image? This is important to know so that, if you're not 100% thrilled with your self-image, at ANY point in your life, you understand where it came from and can discard it and work on a NEW self-image. It really is that easy.

YOU are the creator of your self-image. No one else can take that power from you. And truly, your self-image controls how you behave, whether you succeed or fail, and how others perceive you. And most important, it will determine how happy you are in life. REALLY! IT DOES! True peace and contentment in life comes from knowing you are who you want to be. Even if you've taken the steps to think clearly about who you want to be, and you focus on it, your self-image still controls who you think you are. Let me give you some harmful examples:

<u>Your self-image is a chubby youth that doesn't feel as worthy as the "popular" kids.</u>

> This can cause you to struggle with your weight, lack the confidence that every single person deserves, and keep you from doing things you really would like to do. It may keep you from feeling attractive and worthy of someone's love or respect. It may keep you from dressing the way you really want to, or speaking up when you'd like to, or going after things you'd really like to have or do. That's just the beginning. It's probably keeping you from living.

<u>Your self-image is a rebellious teenager that had to keep your parents from controlling your life.</u>

> This can cause you to go out and get completely wasted, because you think it's cool to do, regardless of the impact on your health or the risk to the rest of your life. It can cause you to be disrespectful at work, or even make it difficult to keep a decent job. You might not care about keeping your home clean. You don't like ANYONE telling you what to do—even if it's a significant other that is just doing it out of love. You stay defensive to, do the opposite of, or try to argue anything the significant people in your life ask you to do. You probably appear to have a chip on your shoulder and hurt those close to you.

<u>Your self-image is an aging, overweight person.</u>

> This can cause you to come up with excuse after excuse as to why you don't exercise or eat better. It can make you feel sick and accept the fact that you "just get sick all the time." It can make you sedentary and lazy, and keep you from trying

anything new. It can frustrate you when you don't grasp something new because you've convinced yourself the old way is better and don't want to change. It can suffocate you and those close to you, and truly make you age faster and allow you to become sick easier.

I think you get the point. Realize what your true self-image is and the damage it can do when it's not completely positive. Understand that it will make you what you are, feel what you do, determine what you do, and control whether you are truly happy inside. When the image is negative at all, it can bring up unrealistic fears you have, and hold you back in life!

Being aware of who you think you are helps you understand why you do what you do, and therefore, helps you change the things you want to change. This is the secret to being your true self and being completely happy with your life. Drop any negative image you have of yourself and replace it with who you really, really want to be. Every single person on earth has this God-given right—to be whoever they want to be. God gave us free will, which means YOU decide who you want to be. This is the key to ultimate happiness.

So take some time to decide who you really want to be. I can't believe any of you would want to be something negative or harmful to yourself or others, so throw any such images away and create a new one. Who is the perfect you? Next, retrain yourself to know that you ARE this person deep down, and you will become it, without fail. Your mind has no option but to follow who you truly think you are, and thus it will behave accordingly. You will automatically cease doing things that are not directly related to your self-image. It's that easy. You may be actively thinking about it, but you will also do some things subconsciously. It's a powerful thing to acknowledge how you've changed, as the more you think about who you are, the faster and stronger your new self will emerge. Once you know it and follow your heart, others will begin seeing it as well, and notice how it changes things for the better for all of you.

I'm asking you to have faith in yourself and try it. What do you have to lose? Even your physical makeup can change. People do this, every day. Body shapes can change, especially if you're overweight. Don't even give me that crap that your genes force you to have a certain body shape! That's an excuse to hold a certain self-image of yourself and states that you've just given up on yourself. And if you believe it, your mind has no choice but to tell your body to be fat. Why do that to yourself? Change your physical self-image and truly want it. Get a picture of yourself in that shape, or pictures of a celebrity or two with that shape, and focus on it, every day, knowing that is the REAL YOU. You will automatically begin making changes in how you care for yourself and seek out methods that can be used to physically change your body. You will even stumble upon things to help you, if you have enough faith. Be attentive to what you're eating, when, and why, and make sure it's good food, because you're hungry, and not some crap because you're emotional or too lazy to plan for a good meal. Decide what your self-image is and go with everything related to it! Every little thing you do goes a long way, so pay attention and use everything to your benefit. For example, if you want to look more like a super model, but think you're too short, there's always options. Work on your core muscles and posture to sit and stand taller, go out and buy yourself some platform or heeled shoes, and look up how to dress for a slimming effect on the internet! Simple.

You may not convince yourself immediately who the new you is, as old habits die hard, and especially when we're stressed or tired, we don't put forth the energy we should for ourselves. So what, if you fall back every now and then? Acknowledge that it doesn't make you feel good and promise yourself you will not be so lazy next time; you will be true to yourself from now on. Depending on your desire and deep belief to change your life for the better, it could take a while to "change over" to your new self-image, or it may happen immediately. It's completely and only up to you. If outside factors throw you back to feeling your old, negative self-image, accept the fact that you're human and realizing it, make at least a small change to prevent it from happening again. You are in full control, both of how you feel about things and how you allow others to treat you. Only you.

Now knock yourself out with a new self image of your ultimate you. Give it some long, hard, serious thought and know you deserve to be who you really want to be. You are short-changing the world until you let the real you come out! But more importantly, you're wasting your valuable life hiding behind something you're not. Time to step out and rise up!

DON'T TREAT YOUR BODY LIKE SH**!

Everything you do has a big impact on your lifespan.

Your body is a machine. What goes in it, is what you'll get out of it. Everything you do to or for your body will take a hit on the condition of your health and your body. Think about it. Why wouldn't it?

Think of another machine, say a car. If you dump sand into a car's gas tank, will it affect the car's performance, gas mileage, and longevity? Of course it does. So why wouldn't you think that when you dump toxins into your body (even sugar, smoke, alcohol, etc.) that it won't affect your performance, energy level, and longevity? Sorry, but the straight-up truth is, it does.

Just like any other machine, the amount and quality of anything that touches your body, such as sleep, food, toxins, and exercise has a direct impact on how you feel, look, and perform (physically and mentally). Did you catch "sleep" in the last sentence? It is important, and it will help determine how long of a life you have. Do yourself a favor and cut back on late nights—be it working, partying, stressing out, or vegging out in front of the stupid tube—and just go to bed in a quiet, dark room and really relax. You'll be surprised how it suddenly becomes easy to think clearly as you're lying there, but also throughout the next day.

It kills me when people complain they're overweight, but refuse to watch how much (quantity) and what (quality) they eat. And the worst of them don't even attempt to get any exercise. What aggravates me even more is when you hear the following conversation between two women:

Woman A: "Oh, you're so lucky you have the body you have. I wish I had a nice figure like you."

Woman B: "You know, I found it really helps to watch the deep-fried or sugary foods and make an effort to eat more vegetables instead."

Woman A: "Ah, I don't think so. That's not for me—how boring! And girl, you have way too much energy!"

Woman B: "Not always. But sometimes I'm good about shutting off the TV at night and getting enough sleep. It's nice to wake up without needing an alarm and taking a walk in the morning."

Woman A: "Ha! You gotta be kidding! That's way too much work for me! Totally boring, again!"

Does Woman A realize her comments are meaningless? Why complain about something you have full control of? If being overweight and overtired is more exciting that being in shape, why exactly is she complaining about it and trying to make Woman B feel guilty because Woman B takes better care of her machine? It's all SH**, once again.

Before I get rolling, let me point out that I don't think dieting is the answer. Life style changes are the answer, if you're not happy with how your machine is looking or performing. Don't freak out! Life style changes do not have to be dramatic or all at once. Every little change helps, just like every time gas goes into a car with little or no sand (aka, a toxin) mixed in.

There are so many things you can do. As far as eating goes, I firmly believe that "everything in moderation" is the key. Too much food is just too much food! It's so simple. If you put more calories, etc. into your pie hole than you're using every day, your body will store the rest and you're gonna gain weight! Think about how much you're eating. Think about why you are eating (I tend to get the munchies when I'm anxious or stressed or bored). Don't inhale your food, don't eat in front of the TV or computer, and for goodness sake, take your time and stop when you're satisfied. We often eat and overeat when we're not even hungry! If you do eat too much, do yourself a favor and get whatever exercise you can, immediately after, as it will help your body handle the excess better than it could if you remain sedentary. Before you put it in your mouth, decide if you want the outcome. If you don't, make a better choice. If you deserve the treat and really want it, go for it, but have no regrets, then.

Everything in moderation also means not eating too much of one type of food, or drinking too much of one drink. Variety is the best way to go. That applies to the good food, the bad food, and the supplements. Don't overdo any one thing. A couple of examples: Too much "low-fat" food can pump in too many carbohydrates and sodium, which just gives you a different problem. Too much protein and not enough carbs can cause another problem. Nothing but all green vegetables will probably leave you with a little more gas (and I'm not talking about the car this time) than you really want! Even herbal and natural supplements are harmful if you take too much! Be leery of jumping on any new diet claims; before long, you'll see newscasts on most of them, telling you about worse side effects. Some of these side effects are suspected to even cause death! Again, ask yourself, is it worth it when a healthy life change would serve you better?

Now before you focus on just your body, I need to give you the key to making it all work. Your body WILL follow what your mind thinks. The healthier and happier and more convinced the mind is, the easier it will be to get the body to cooperate. It must be on board before you will succeed and get to your "ideal body." First of all, you MUST have a self-image of what you really, truly want to look like, down to the details of the shape and firmness of every part of your body. Notice I didn't say anything about how much you weigh, as the pounds don't matter. The way you want your body and muscles to be shaped is what matters. Pull out a picture of yourself when you looked like that, or edit a photo, or gather up photos that you have to see every day, so that deep down, you KNOW what you want to look like and that you will look like that soon.

For me, it had to have a picture of my head on it to get myself to believe it, so it was easiest to pull out pictures of myself from years ago when I was a lighter, more fit person. I also tried to keep pictures I'd seen in magazines nearby, when a particular part of the model's body was what I wanted for me. I needed to have the image in my head and picture it on my body. I also had to read about and believe that the body can basically reconstruct itself, over and over, based on what your mind knows and wants. The mind also helps to remind you to think before you eat and to get a variety of exercise, whenever you can. Forget all the negative bull that you've ever heard about gaining weight as you get older, or as you have kids, etc. If this happened to you, it was only because you believed it would, deep down (and you probably ate and drank accordingly and actually made yourself gain weight). Your mind will direct your body, good or bad, according to what you truly believe. If what you see right now as your self-image is not what you wanted, CHANGE IT immediately! (Refer to the chapter, "What is Your Self Image?")

Once you have the mind engaged, there's a ton of books out there on a healthy lifestyle, and tons more on the internet, so I'm not going into it too deep here, because most people have a good idea of good and bad eating and drinking habits. I'll toss out some of the obvious ones, though:

1. Water is probably the most important thing you can give your body! It keeps everything working and flushes out the junk. Drink lots of plain water, every day. The recommendations vary, based on your age and weight, but at least a few good-sized glasses of plain water every day is good for just about any kid or adult. I've heard you're supposed to take your weight in pounds and divide it in half. That number is the number of ounces of PLAIN water you are supposed to have, on a normal day. Obviously, if you're

doing anything that may dehydrate you, you should add to this quantity of plain water accordingly.

2. Vitamin-enriched water is a much better choice than soda and most fruit juices, but you still need a lot of plain water every day. If you buy enriched water, read the label first for sugar, sodium, carbohydrates, etc. because it could have more bad stuff than good in it!

3. Stress works against your body, in all areas. Address and release the stress, first and foremost. Bonus: Exercise will almost always help you relieve some stress.

4. Deep-fried foods are usually the worst foods for you.

5. Alcohol, drugs, and smoking are toxins and make the body work very hard (like sand in your tank) and will shorten your lifespan, without a doubt.

6. Unprocessed foods (fresh foods) are usually better than processed foods (boxed, canned, frozen, etc.)

7. Read the label before buying or eating for things you should limit! Anything high in the following areas is usually not very healthy: caffeine, sugar, calories, fat, sodium, carbohydrates, etc.

8. Read the label before buying, for things that are good for you. If it doesn't have any nutritional

value, reconsider. Many things will surprise you, because they don't have an ounce of nutrition in them! Obviously, you're looking for vitamins, minerals, proteins, fiber, etc. Look for things heavy on nutrition and light on the bad things mentioned in the previous section for your ideal foods or drinks. And please check out the drinks! Most fruit juices have little or no nutritional value and so many bad things in them. Sometimes they're as bad as soda! If in doubt, make your own juice from fresh fruits and vegetables.

9. If you have some favorite restaurants, they will often have the food labels available on the internet. Just knowing what's in the food helps you make the best choices for what you want out of your body.

10. Diet remedies of most types DO have side effects. Don't fool yourself into thinking that any one of them is completely safe. Respect your body, reminding yourself it is the ONLY ONE you will have in this lifetime. If you consume something that is later discovered to contribute to causing cancer, will it have been worth it? And most likely, it won't really work without your changing your lifestyle, anyway. Yeah, I've seen all the "look what it did for me!" claims too. What they don't mention is that the person also increased their exercise and/or changed their eating habits along with it, and that lifestyle change is what really made a difference.

11. Every bit of exercise you get moves your machine and does make a difference. If you

want to firm up, lose weight, and have more energy, you need to exercise according to your goals. Even exercising one day a week instead of no days will make a difference, but if you want a bigger alteration, exercise more than that. You know the basics here. If you're moving, it's exercise. For me, a 30-minute walk, three times a week is the best. First thing in the morning, after a glass of water, seems to be the most effective for me.

12. Exercise works your outside, but your inside too! Remember, you have critical organs keeping your body moving. The heart, lungs, digestive system, blood flow, etc. all gets the exercise too, so it'll help keep them all performing too! Not to mention the muscle strength and flexibility. I could go on and on, but again, pros have written plenty on this.

13. Too much of anything—even exercise—is still not good. Don't get me wrong, I'm not trying to give you an excuse for not exercising. Let's say you do the same exercise, everyday, and the muscles you're working are pumped up really nice. That's great, but realize that when you stop working them, they're gonna turn to flab. Also, your muscles are smart, and will stop being affected by that particular exercise very much, after a while. You want to vary your exercise routines for the most benefit. I also believe that it's good to let the muscles rest and rebuild and not work the same ones every day. Again, your specific goals come first, but keep it in mind.

Just a little simple thought before you partake in something can keep you from beating up your poor body. Think, "Is what I'm about to do or doing now REALLY what's best for me?" If not, think, "Why am I doing it?" Also pay attention to how your body feels during and after it. Listen to your body! If whatever you did doesn't make it feel wonderful, then it's probably not the best thing for your body. This includes exercise! Done the right way, it should NOT hurt! Sometimes we do things without thinking, for very simple reasons, like boredom, anxiety, or being social, but if it isn't something that you really wanted, then cease doing it, or scale back as much as you can. You'll be very happy you did, and your body (and then, your mind and soul) will be even happier.

PUT A LITTLE EFFORT INTO YOU!

 **If you're not at 100%, you can't do your best. Strive for 100%.**

As I mentioned earlier, this entire book is based on my opinions and my ideas. I've formed these opinions over time, obviously, based on my experiences, observations, and information I've found in various places. I am not a doctor. I do not have all of life's answers. I can only relay what I have learned through either personal experience or the experience of someone I know. As always, always choose what is best for you!

To live the best life possible, you have to pay a little attention to yourself. It's only when you are operating at your best condition that you can give your best to others, and to what you want in your life. I focus a lot on mental and emotional issues throughout this book, but it's important to pay close attention to your physical condition, as well. Once again, if you're not functioning at 100 percent in mind, body, and soul, how can you do your best?

While this particular section is focused on the body, I want to recap mind and soul, briefly. Remember, positive emotions, thoughts, and actions promote health and happiness; negative emotions, thoughts, and actions deteriorate the body, mind, and soul. In addition, your free will and focus will drive what happens in your life and with your body as well. If you wake up often dreading the day, thinking life is hard and questioning if it's worth it, your free will is asking for relief from it, like, leaving this life! Be careful where you let your primary thoughts go!

The state of your mind and soul have even more power than the body, but being the vehicle that will carry you through this entire life, you must give your physical state equal attention. Take care of your body. Exercise, eat right, avoid toxins, and pay attention to and research whatever you can about any little ailment you might have. Make being healthy your first priority. If you have a medical issue, don't discard your responsibility to yourself by putting everything into the hands of the doctors. Do your own digging, especially on the internet, where all kinds of ideas and options are presented.

I firmly believe that anything the body does, healthy or sick, is a result of more than one thing the body has been exposed to. Disease, for instance. While a lot of people are exposed to the same things, or have the same genes, why do only some get the disease? When the flu goes around, why do some people get it, and some don't? Why do some get it worse than others? My common sense tells me, it's the combination of something in the body. If you have the exact right combination, bingo! The disease has a hit and can settle itself in. If it does not have the exact right combination, it does not affect you, or affects **you** very little, perhaps to the degree you don't even notice it. I think this applies to everything, from the common cold, to allergies, and to worse diseases and cancer.

So, if it IS a combination that allows the sickness to set in, it makes sense that removing something in the combination of things that the sickness needs to support itself will cause it to diminish and disappear, doesn't it? Moreover, something else that is introduced may make one of the ingredients ineffective or less effective, and counter-act the perfect combination. Makes sense, doesn't it? How else can we explain people that reverse deadly diseases, even some times without the recommended medical treatment? And most times of course, the recommended medical treatment is the thing that counter-acts the combination. But sometimes, the medical treatment alone is not enough. Sometimes the combination is quite complex and you have to attack it from all sides. Moreover, if you don't remove the key ingredient that is allowing the disease to flourish, all the medicine in the world won't be able to completely overpower it. Is this starting to make sense?

FACTORS AND COMBINATIONS THAT CAN DETERMINE YOUR HEALTH:

1. Stress and negativity. You should know by now that any is harmful.

2. Frame of mind or level of contentment.

3. Nutrition, including too much of something that is otherwise healthy, or the lack of any of the required food group quantities.

4. Lack of sleep. Seriously, leave the TV off and just go to sleep!

5. Lack of exercise, which not only determines what the outside of your body looks like, but the

inside as well. We all know exercise keeps the organs and internal systems in shape, but also benefits brain power, body chemistry, longevity, etc.

6. Injuries, even the ones we don't notice or the ones that can't be diagnosed by the medical doctors, directly, like scar tissue and kinked-up nerves and soft tissue. These can cause an extreme amount of pain, help you predict weather changes, and quickly disable you for the day, without any warning. For some stupid reason, society has accepted the statement, "It's just something you'll have to live with." What a bunch of bullSH**! There is always something out there to help, and you wouldn't believe what the right trained professional can do with re-training soft tissue to do its job, relax stressed or pinched nerves, and allow your body to regenerate healthy cells and quite possibly, permanently relieve your pain! Sure, health insurance doesn't always cover these types of treatments, but for my body, I'll pay a little out of my own pocket to have my body permanently fixed! Realize that if the glue that holds a part of the body is not stable, it can move on to damaging many other parts of your body, whether they're connected to it directly, or the result of you overcompensating to work around the soreness.

7. Exposure to smoke, any kind of fumes, or anything in the air, including perfumes, hairspray, cleaner scents, candle scents, and air fresheners.

8. Medications, including herbal and vitamin supplements, etc. Make sure you know that all the possible side effects are before you consume anything! Don't just throw a pain reliever at it, find the source of the problem and correct it! You hear and read all the time how both prescribed medications and supplements cause awful side effects and worse problems than the reason someone started taking them! Now if it's a critical medication, you need to keep the doctor informed and work on your own and with them to research all other possible options. But don't be careless and put all of the responsibility into the doctor's hands. Only you know what your body is feeling. If you value your health at all, you should be the number one expert on you and your ailments—not your doctor! Medicine is not an exact science, but often detective work, as everyone's body and conditions and contributors are different—no two people are alike. In addition, no one person knows it all! The medical doctors know a piece of it, while chiropractors specialize in another area, in addition to massage/nerve treatment specialists that focus on the nerve endings and soft tissues of your body. Others may know more about allergies, exercise, nutrition, etc. Don't think that all you can do is go to the medical doctors! Work with a team of doctors and specialists, to explore all options, including the wellness treatments available, outside of the standard medical network. Keep working on it until you treat all of the pieces that might be contributing to your problem. Don't give up! Someone out there has a solution for you. There are so many options out there, it makes your head spin, but

the internet sure makes it easy to research just about anything, and to talk to others with the same symptoms. It is not uncommon to find someone that has found a solution to your problem. Do your research because this is the only body you get.

9. Toxins in anything we consume by eating, drinking, smelling. Preservatives, artificial food additives, residue from dishwashing soap or the cleaners we used on our counter, metals from cookware or cans we drink out of, or even too much of somewhat "safe" things like sugar, caffeine, alcohol.

10. Toxins on food, even raw foods, like insecticides, pesticides, waxes, etc. At least organic foods don't use as much of this stuff, and none at all, if it's true organic. Local produce stands and farmers markets often offer good organic stuff. Once you taste the difference, you'll be hooked. Natural does not mean organic, but could have benefits over processed foods. Make sure you are in the habit of reading labels, but keep in mind, not everything appears on the label! Grow whatever of your own food that you can. That way, you know what's in it and you can have the best-tasting and most nutritious fruits and vegetables possible.

11. Toxins in anything that touches our skin, not just household cleaners, but things we use to clean our clothes, including dryer sheets and static sprays (the sprays are awful for inhaling too!), lotions, oils, soaps, shampoos, and antiperspirants with aluminum. Articles have

been published, warning people of the research that proves that some household cleaners leave residue behind, even after it's dry that's harsh enough to burn the skin (some floor cleaners, for instance), and therefore, poison you through absorption by your skin, or poison food (on the counters). Also, I know more than a couple of people who get rashes from some or most of the antiperspirants on the market. A simple switch to a different brand, or one without aluminum resolved the problem of the rash, swelling, and even feeling nauseous!

12. Toxins created when things are exposed to temperature extremes, like water heating up in a plastic bottle or container (in your microwave or your hot car) or water freezing in a plastic container. Many believe that any sort of plastic in the microwave releases toxins into the food contained in it when you heat it up. Makes sense to me, so I try my best not to use anything containing plastic in the microwave—plates, bowls, plastic wrap, etc. Why risk it when there is scientific evidence to prove the toxins are released?

Now if you have been ignoring any of the things on this list, as most of us do, realize that is it so incredibly easy to change a lot without inconveniencing anyone. I'm not asking you to freak out and restrict you and your household from touching anything on the list, I'm just asking you to think twice about what you do, and do what's safest and healthiest for everyone. Just pay attention to a couple of things at a time and explore how you can change to a healthier method. Anything is better than nothing, right? Even if you don't believe all the documented facts on the items above, why would you take the risk, when someone tells you over and over it may not be safe? Is your life really that bad, that you want to help get it over with, sooner? If so, I would suspect that you aren't pursuing a meaningful purpose in your life then, so please read the rest of this book and get started! Moreover, if you don't take care of yourself for you, maybe you could do it for the people that care about you? Think it over! Again, there are SO many resources out there, documenting the dangers and the healthy alternatives available, so I don't need to try to dive into those deep subjects, but most of it is just common sense.

Everything in moderation (assuming it's safe to start with), and always, listen to your body, for your own sake! The occasional aches and pains you wake up with are a huge sign that you overindulged in something the day before that your body doesn't like. These are the easiest to figure out. Are you super tired and need a little more sleep, either because you've short-changed it lately, or because your body might be fighting something? Well, see what you can do about getting to bed earlier. Do you feel swollen, congested, and dehydrated? You might have had too much sugar or something. Are your lymph nodes swollen and achy? You might have had too much caffeine. Maybe you had too much of something the day before and not nearly enough water? That's common. Try to drink lots of plain water before bedtime and right after you wake up to help flush it all out. Food intolerances can also trigger almost instant stomach bloating and cramps, and even congestion and digestive problems. Pay attention and eliminate or limit that food from now on! Your body is telling you it does not like it or a combination of it. It doesn't take a genius, just someone that cares about themselves. It is the only body you're gonna have, this time around. Are you gonna be happy with yourself, when you're 70-something years old and can't eat a thing, because you ignored your body asking you to stop eating or drinking just one or two things, for years?

Now obviously, we have those long-term ailments, too. These need more attention, though they could be coming from many of the same sources. You also might have an injury or issue that will continue to worsen, if you don't pay attention to resolving it. Don't you think it'd be easier to get rid of the problem before it's life-threatening? Think of all the money you save taking care of it now, versus having to be hospitalized? You can avoid a lot by just giving a little thought to your health. Obviously, you should engage in healthy behavior and see if it resolves it on its own, through all the things I talk about in that section of this book. But maybe that doesn't do it, on its own. Remember, the options for solutions are endless! Do some research and seek out experts and specific books or articles on your problem. Decide which safe methods you would like to try and try them, one at a time, so you know what works. Don't give up! It's you and your loved ones that you'd be giving up on!

And please, whatever you do, don't listen to the lethally negative people (even doctors!) that say, "You have a disease. You need to accept it." Those comments only make you focus on and talk about the disease more, instead of talking about getting healthy again. You must have health and solutions as the primary focus of your mind in order to heal yourself! Your free will actually has the power to perform miracles, if you let it. You must see yourself completely healthy and happy and feel the gratitude of it to find healing. Once you decide how you want your life to be, there's nothing holding you back from finding the solutions, or even miracles, to get back to being stronger than you've ever been. Stay in control and do what is best for you!

I'll emphasize again, the culprit could be a single thing, or it may be a combination of things, like different things you are ingesting, absorbing, or breathing. It could be an injury you had, or a combination of the injury along with the snowball effect of neglecting it.

For instance, I broke my neck a few years back. The bones healed great but the soft tissue and nerves were left out-of-whack. Physical therapy didn't work, but chiropractic adjustments and massage provided temporary relief. With the relief, I started exercising and strengthening my weakened areas, but I continued to have symptoms. Headaches, kinks, shooting pain, numbness, fatigue, and low energy seem to pounce on me from nowhere, despite all my efforts to keep my body flexible and in shape. All the experts told me, it was just something I'd have to live with. I didn't believe them for years, but tired and feeling defeated, I started to accept it.

What a mistake, and a dumb thing to do! All my symptoms got worse and worse, where soon, there were very few days I could even exercise much. I knew better, but hearing the negative statement over and over again had moved my focus to it. You should never adopt society's comments and beliefs, unless you feel it is very beneficial to you. If it is negative or harmful, disregard it, as it does you no good. It serves no benefit to you, so ignore what everybody else says and what everybody else does. Do only what's best for you!

Then, thank God, I ran into someone I haven't seen in years, who noticed my gingerly handling of the weights at the gym. He asked if I was feeling okay and I explained. He insisted I go to an expert he visits, to work on retraining my soft tissue to do their job. He reminded me that the body is capable of healing itself, whatever the issue. I knew he was right, but even still, I didn't go see him right away, since the costs wouldn't be covered by insurance. Maybe too, I was hoping that I could get rid of the negative thoughts that were keeping me from getting my full strength back and do it on my own. Well, whether my focus wasn't there or whether I just needed an expert's help to fix it, I finally got tired of not being at 100 percent, and went and saw the guy.

Within two visits, I was positive this was the solution to fix my body, permanently. Nearly everything went away or was significantly better! I felt so great! So much so, I finally realized how much pain and inconvenience I had been trying to live with. What a difference, especially in my energy level! All I needed was a couple of simple "active release" sessions to retrain my soft tissue. Now I had never heard of this method before, but I can't help but think that my thoughts on having my healthy, strong body back is what created the chance meeting, and advice from, the only way I might have heard about it! The moral of the story? Keep looking, keep thinking, and never give up!

Be determined, use some common sense and the process of elimination for everything to weed out the possible culprits. Remove, reduce, or replace <u>one thing at a time for a week</u>, or less if you can tell right away. Remember to work with your doctor when it comes to critical, prescribed medications, but remember, that's just one thing that can be causing the problem. In addition, introduce healthier habits to counteract what's going on.

Look at my previous list of factors and start your detective work. You can certainly change a bunch of things at once, but then you won't know what resolved your problem, necessarily. But then again, that's not really important. What's important is that you resolved the issue. Remember, plenty of people have written plenty of proven research on all of the topics I listed. Do your own thinking and analyzing based on the facts and the interaction you have with others that have found solutions. Use the vast information on the internet. Get ideas and referrals from family and friends. Keep a quick journal of what you're doing and how you're feeling so that you can see the patterns and look back at it, when you or a professional needs to. It also comes in handy if you end up being the advisor to someone else, later.

Just like I encourage you, or rather, lecture you, to think through other things, I feel even stronger that you need to listen to your body and make the effort to get to the source of the problem and correct it. Value yourself more than to just throw an easy, temporary fix at it. Maybe it'll make you feel better today, but don't you want to feel good tomorrow too? I know it's a lengthy list, but it gives you plenty of options, doesn't it? And I'm sure there's more that I haven't even touched on. Paying attention to, or changing just one of those ingredients may be all it takes! Isn't your health and feeling good worth it? Isn't doing what you want with your life worth it? Give yourself a fair chance by going at it 100 percent!

WHERE DO I BELONG?

Trust your true feelings to guide you to your destiny in life.

Most people, at some point in there life, struggle to find their perfect place in the universe. Some try very little to think about it; they live in denial through most of their years. Some hit crisis or tragedies or near-death experiences and take a few moments to ponder. Some search for it their whole life, and never find it. But at some point, if we're very honest with ourselves, we wonder, where do I belong?

I like to think of the world as a puzzle. Every single body brought into this world is one of the pieces of the puzzle. If every single person is where they belong (who they should be), the puzzle is complete—it is perfect. Everyone is linked in harmony and the beauty of the puzzle is displayed.

The struggle most everyone faces is trying to find their place; until they are in their perfect place, ultimate self-content and peace is merely a dream. We move around the puzzle board, often trying to fit in to the wrong place. Everything we do, every day, has some effect on finding our place in the puzzle. If we are quite passive and just "go with the flow" we basically sit in the same place; we don't make any effort in finding our ideal place in the puzzle. If we live a selfish life, we move away from our perfect place. Every negative action we take moves us farther and farther from where we are meant to be. But we are rewarded for every positive impact we have on others and on ourselves. Every time we do something good, we move towards finding our perfect place in that same measure.

We may get to a place that we believe we might fit in, and so we try it on. If the fit is completely wrong, we know fairly quickly because it does not make us feel good. How we feel is a very easy, no-fault way to know if we're in or near our "right spot." If it gives us a negative feeling, we are not in the right place or doing the right thing. It's really quite simple. I truly believe that doing something that's bad for us or bad for others will never make us feel good; it is the wrong place in the universe—the wrong place in the puzzle.

Sometimes we find a place that's fairly comfortable. The edges seemingly line up and we can squeeze into that spot. But then after a while, we feel uncomfortable and have to pull out of place, once again. Sometimes we take the time to make ourselves aware of what's right, and we put the effort into it during that time. Perhaps there are other people or influences in your life that make this an easy spot to sit in. This is when we feel good about our "place in the puzzle." But eventually, we feel like there's something more we should be doing. We suspect there may be more that we're capable of, and the comfort doesn't last. It doesn't mean you were not meant to be in that spot for a while—you probably were supposed to rest in that comfort for a while and learn more about yourself—learn more about how you line up. The others that are around you at that time also benefited from your being in that place. It helps them to learn how to continue to help others, until they too, find the pieces that match up with their "edges." It helps everyone to recognize what is needed to complete the puzzle and what pieces or empty spots to look for.

Remember that the puzzle is all linked together. So if you are trying to fit into a spot not meant for you, you are affecting all the other pieces around you. It's never just about you. The universe is the universe, and we cannot change that. Everything and everyone is linked together, somehow. Yes, there are pieces on the other side of the puzzle that you may never come in contact with, but they can't achieve perfect harmony or experience the perfect world unless EVERYONE is in their proper place. EVERYONE includes you. That is the wonderful fact. You were born to fill a spot, and to be fulfilled, in the world. Everyone was born to fill their proper spot.

So without everyone in their proper place, should we give up hope? Well, think about it. Picture yourself working on a terribly complicated puzzle. If you find two pieces that link together, don't you feel some satisfaction? It is the same with the world. If you help just one other person, BOTH of you feel contentment. Now, if you continue on and find more and more pieces, you could end up putting an entire section together. While all pieces are not linked directly to you, you are still part of making that section complete, and you probably helped make the connection to the other pieces. Now, you actually get a glimpse of what that part of the puzzle portrays. Part of the mystery is exposed and everyone connected to it feels the harmony. Moreover, other pieces of the puzzle observe what is happening and strive to connect as well. If you or any of the other pieces pull out, there is fear, and literally, a hole of emptiness. The section is incomplete without you. Every single person is necessary to display the real beauty of the puzzle, or at least a section of the puzzle. That is how important you are. That is how important everyone around you is. Treat yourself (and others) with the respect you deserve.

If you are nearing the right section, the combined effort of the people in the spaces around you will bring guidance, joy, love, and everything that's positive and fulfilling in life. If you are nearing or in the wrong section or place, there will be discontent, chaos, sadness, and all that's negative and evil in life. Not only will you send out these feelings and actions of discord, but those around you will also close in on you. The world will literally kick your ass, some days. You will feel like everything is against you, and truly, it is. That area of the puzzle does not want you trying to place yourself where you don't belong. That space is for someone else, not you. The sooner you move away from it, the better. In these cases, it is better to float around the outside border of the puzzle than to be in the way of other pieces that belong there. At least you'll be free to find another spot.

So sometimes we do float around the puzzle, lost and lonely, not knowing where to go next. Have faith. There is a perfect spot for you. It is just sitting there, waiting for you. You can find your way by trusting your feelings. Anything that makes your heart feel full and free is telling you, you are headed in the right direction, towards where you are meant to be. Anything that makes you feel empty, embarrassed, regretful, etc. is telling you, you are headed directly away from where you're supposed to be going. So listen to your feelings and let it guide you. When you realize you're headed the wrong way, apologize to others and to YOURSELF, and then continue looking for your place. It is still there, waiting for you. Let other people around you help you learn and feel at peace, and try to do the same for them; they are probably part of your section of the puzzle. But always remember, your section of the puzzle doesn't close up because you headed in the wrong direction, temporarily. The sooner you turn around, the sooner you can stop moving away from your perfect spot. Know that it will ALWAYS be there waiting for you. You are the only person that fits into that spot.

THINK, PLAY, AND DREAM LIKE YOU DID AS A CHILD

 **Children know what it's all about. Learn from them, to be real again.**

I think the most disappointing thing a person can do to themselves and the rest of the world is to turn into a typical adult. Responsibilities and demands make people crabby as they encounter a new part of their life. Then, even when you're on your own time, you're stressed, depressed, worrisome, tired, restrained, and cranky. What a waste of life! You are suffocating yourself! You've clipped your own wings. That's enough to bum anybody out!

But it wasn't always that way. Childhood is filled with smiles, playing, innocent dreams, and open expressions. You weren't afraid to go after something, to ask for anything, and to show your affection. Nothing was impossible, especially when you "got big enough" to call your own shots. Well, you are big enough now, so what happened?

Some will say reality set in and childish dreams are foolish, but I wholeheartedly disagree. Sadly, I think this is just an excuse from holding yourself accountable for your life and what it's become. As an adult, we gain full control over our lives and how we behave, and what we go after; but we stop ourselves. Why? Even if our dreams evolved or changed over time, or even if we came up with new dreams, it's still something we desire a tremendous amount. So why make it remain just a dream? Scoff if you will, but I dare you to read on, then.

Quite simply, I truly believe that everything we do (or not do) comes out of one of two emotions: FEAR or LOVE. Fear is anything that you are afraid of, obviously. Love is anything that comes from deep down within your heart as being the thing that will make you feel most fulfilled. Now you might have to think about this a little, and dig in to the root of things, to see which you are using to make your choices.

For instance, let's say you tried skiing when you were 10 years old and you fell and broke your leg, and you remember quite vividly the pain and recovery, along with the teasing from your classmates when you struggled to hobble around school. So after that, you never went skiing again, even though you'd like to try it again. FEAR from a past memory made that decision for you, on several counts, from worrying that people would think you couldn't do it, to the fear of being hurt again. If you're content with never trying it again, fine, but if you secretly desire to get out there and conquer the ski hill, choose with your heart and go try it!

A similar case could be made for someone who just heard about your fall and decided then and there to never attempt to ski. This person has the FEAR of what could happen, not even of what did happen to them, in the past. Fear, not love for themselves and what they really want, holds them back. Emotionally, too many people hold themselves back for the very same reasons. Fear of something that happened in the past, fear of something that could possibly happen, and even fear of the unknown of all crazy things, keeps most adults in a chokehold.

You can apply this simple analysis of why you choose what you do to ANYTHING, ANYTIME. All it takes is a minute of thought. All it takes is for you to make a commitment to yourself as to what you will use to choose. You will find that no matter the outcome, when you choose with your heart, or out of love, you just can't go wrong. Even if the very worst happens, you know you proceeded with good intentions, and at least you tried. You will not feel defeated or disappointed, as you do when you choose with fear.

Thinking first, and choosing with love versus fear may take you some practice, as old habits die hard. But know that the more you practice it, the easier and more natural it becomes. You quickly feel content, at peace, and even elated. Moreover, your example shines bright on anyone around you, encouraging them to do the same. It's all good! Oh, and the fun you will have!

Along with this, you have to learn to leave negative memories in the past, instead of letting them pile up in your bag of fears. Time is there to serve us in growing wiser, not in growing a pile of SH** that we drag around! We can control choosing with love, no matter what may be in our past. We probably learned something from the past experiences, but it wasn't supposed to teach us to refrain from wanting and living our dreams. Past SH** is meant to stay in the past!

Don't drag it around and smother yourself to the point you that can't move or breathe anymore!

Let the attitude you had as child come out, whenever and wherever you are choosing with your heart. From little things, like jumping on a swing on a playground again, to big things like going after the life you really want to live, you'll have no regrets leaving the crabby, unenergetic, boring adult with the big bag of SH** behind. Trust me. You might even learn how to giggle again.

FIND HARMONY!

**Harmony is natural.
Small-minded thinking is not.**

Human nature makes us quick to judge others that are different from us, and leads towards a tendency to have a small mind, when it comes to understanding and tolerating those with opposing opinions, lifestyles, or beliefs. We tend to dwell on what makes us different, and sometimes we even get angry about those differences.

Negative feelings towards others makes for an ugly encounter and it brings out the ugliness in you, and instead of harmony, you cause chaos and bad vibes. On the opposite end, the world rocks and people grow when there is unity and common goals. But how do we get there, when we're so different?

It's easy; simply expand your mind and change the way you think. I'm not saying you should change your opinions to theirs, just change your focus, and you can change the entire situation. Instead of thinking about what's different and what they do that you don't like, think about what is the same, or common, and thus, what you can see eye to eye on. You know there has to be something, if you just take a moment to think about it.

Let's start with a coworker. Maybe you don't like the way they do a lot of personal things during work time, including office gossip. Maybe you don't like their lifestyle away from work. Maybe it starts to wear on you, and makes you less productive at work. That hardly seems like it benefits you. Remember, you are the one in control of how it affects you.

So forget about all the stuff you don't like, and think about what you do like about this person, for instance, their work is thorough and on-time. They rarely call in sick, and they handle some work for you, when you're out. You both have a common goal of getting the work done, so there is harmony there. Appreciate that common ideal that you both have, and focus on that. You are at work, after all, and work should be your primary focus. Who cares what they do, outside of that?

Another common stress point occurs between family members, especially as the family matures and siblings begin to live their own life. You may not always like the way your brothers or sisters act or think, or perhaps even some choices they make in lifestyles, spouses, and attitudes towards others in the family. On the other hand, you may agree on many things, for instance, on how your parents will be taken care of in their old age, or that celebrating the holidays together is important, or perhaps you have mutual friends.

Again, focus on what you DO have in common and appreciate that as the glue that binds you together and let them live their own life. It's not your job to keep them from making mistakes or to force them to live the way you think they should. You grew up together and have shared some good times. Keep that foremost in your mind and you'll create a positive environment for the whole family and walk away feeling good about being the bigger person.

Harmony doesn't come from people being the same, and it doesn't have to mean that people "click." It means that through flexible and sometimes creative thinking, you can come together and coexist with others to reach a common goal, or at least tolerate each other to allow others to achieve a greater goal. Think of the beautiful music that is formed when people harmonize. Even though each person is singing their own unique and different note, when they sing the notes together, at the same time and at equal volumes, something spectacular emerges. The very different notes form a sound unlike anything that could be produced on its own. All parts of the very different sounds are required, and required to join together at the perfect moment to evolve into that wonderful sound! Moreover, it sounds best when all are using the same volume, versus one being louder and overpowering the rest. If one is too loud, you can't hear the other sounds, thus the truest harmony is not achieved.

It works the same way with people. We need each other's uniqueness, input, and cooperation to build the really great stuff and to reach our mutual goals, sometimes. Keep the end mission in mind and focus on it instead of the nit-picky other junk that just doesn't matter. Give it a try. Harmony is always there, just dying to come out. All you have to do is peel away the weak negative layer to get to it. It's just dying to come out.

We are all here for a reason. We are all meant to work together and help each other out. Our differences are what makes each of us beautifully unique. So you see, judging or disliking other people's differences is a very silly thing to waste your time on, don't you think? Find something better to do and allow your mind to do its rightful job. Let your mind focus on what you can achieve together. Allow the positive outcome to occur. Let harmony have a chance, because honestly, that's how it supposed to be.

DON'T HESITATE TO SHOW YOU CARE, APPRECIATE, OR LOVE

Show your positive emotions every chance you get.

Very often, we don't tell people how we really feel, even when it's a wonderful, no-way-to-lose feeling like caring, appreciation, or love. Why is that? It's crazy, isn't it?

I can only go back to knowing that all actions or lack of action or choices are made out of one of two emotions: Love or Fear. It really is that simple, and it can be very easy to remember, when you're contemplating something. Are you choosing what you are out of love or fear? Before making the decision, make sure you recall that if choices are made out of love, you can't go wrong. Choices made out of fear are what we'd call the "wrong" choices and they will likely have a negative impact on you and anyone else affected. Think this through before making your choice and you'll think more clearly.

I bring this up because I feel that withholding expressions of the wonderful emotions can only come from a fear of something. It could be any of the following fears: fear of rejection, fear of being vulnerable, fear of being taken advantage of, but mostly, I think it's a fear of opening yourself up. On the other hand, if you think with love, either for yourself or the people you care about, a wonderful feeling will resonate somewhere. Even if you stick your heart out and admit to someone you love them, and the feeling isn't mutual, would you have been satisfied if you hadn't tried at all? No, you wouldn't, because you would have let yourself down. And this is the "worst case scenario" possible, yet you still come out unscarred, and you are free to move on. You can be proud of your choice to express your emotions. Moreover, when the love of your life is standing before you, waiting to hear you say you love them, you will have had the practice and not fear doing so. It will come naturally.

Don't worry, expression doesn't always have to be fireworks and hearts bursting. They can come at any level or gesture. While telling someone outright ensures they will know how you feel (through any means, like talking, writing, or a message on a card or gift), it's certainly not the only way to let them know. There are a million ways to show people you care. As I just mentioned, the most obvious is through spoken or written words, but actions carry almost as much of a positive impact, depending on the situation. Gestures, actions, effort. There are countless ways to express yourself through your actions.

Here's a few examples:

- Holding hands
- Hugs
- Backrubs
- A Pat the back

- Doing favors
- Helping with chores or errands
- Making a snack/meal
- Opening a door
- Making a random phone call just to ask how they are
- Being goofy to make them smile
- Driving up to a door when it's cold or raining
- Leaving a note or sending a text or email
- Giving them a card that says how you feel
- Gifts (can be very small, and customized; handmade makes the biggest impact!)
- Kisses!
- Saying thank you
- Asking how they feel or how their day was
- Surprises
- Anything, anything, anything to let them know they are appreciated or special to you!

It takes so much less effort to just let those positive expressions out, versus battling with your fears to find an excuse not to. Go with what your warm heart wants and with what makes you feel good. The bonus? You'll have no regrets and likely, something wonderful will evolve that could not have come about, had you listened to your fears. Try it. You'll like it!

SAVOR!

You are cheating yourself, if you don't take time to enjoy the good things.

Some things are meant to be savored, not gulped up without thinking! You will enjoy life more, if you just slow down a little and allow yourself to indulge. Think of the "S" in savor, and it'll be easy.

-Sustenance (food and drink). Take the time to really TASTE what you're putting in your mouth, and don't salt or sauce the crap out of so it tastes like salt or sauce. Trust me, if you take the time, you will enjoy every little thing you consume, thus you will make better selections and tend to not overindulge. Don't just mindlessly stuff your pie hole for something to do, to find comfort, or to handle anxiety!

-Sleep. First of all, keep the TV, computer, and mobile devices shut off when it's getting close to bedtime! When you're tired and it's time for bed, just go to bed to sleep, instead of filling your brain with mindless stuff! Let yourself relax, think about the good things of the day, and about a perfect tomorrow. If you're as busy as most people, this is critical, as it's difficult to have any time at all in the day to think clearly. Just before you go to sleep is the ideal time to think about the things that make your life perfect, as your mind will continue working on these things while you sleep.

-Sensual moments with your special somebody. Okay, you say this is a no-brainer. So tell me why people don't do it more often? Especially (and most importantly) with someone they love? It is one of the most gratifying, relaxing, healthy things you can do, for both you and your sweetie! Take some time to do it, in little portions or in lengthy portions whenever possible, and to do it right with lots of feeling, for crime-anny sakes!

-Scenery. Ahhhh. We are so blessed to have such gorgeous nature and man-made wonders all around us, wherever we go. Instead of driving by or walking around in your own little tunnel, take a moment to look and smile at something beautiful. It will make you feel better—I promise!

-Spirit. We all have our own inner self—our own unique spirit. It is there to be appreciated by everyone, but most importantly, yourself. Nuture it and let it grow and expand. It's amazing what we are all stifling with our closed minds. You are responsible for yourself, but also the spirits you come in contact with. No spirit is meant to exist by itself—it advances to a larger realm by connecting with another, be it people or God. Be kind to others and set a wonderful example of what a happy life feels like, so they can confidently pursue it, too. In addition, most people believe the spirit never dies—just changes form (like when we die), so it does matter how you live your life. Personally, I do believe it's not over when your body dies, so I'm gonna try to take good care of my spirit and expand all I can before this life is over!

-Smiles! Smile. Why not? It makes you feel good. It makes other people feel good. It might even lead to laughter and change someone's day; it might even change your day. Those face muscles were meant to be used, not to droop into a permanent scowl. Nobody likes a crabby pants, so why bother! Why not smile?

-Scratch the surface. I've only scratched the surface and pointed out some of the things we have been given that were obviously meant to make us feel good, to be savored, and to be appreciated. If you let yourself, I bet you can come up with many more, right now. Look around you, as you go through your day and you'll discover that you're missing a whole lot that you could be enjoying. Even right now.

So get started. You have no excuse. Live every moment the way God intended and be continuously amazed at what else He has waiting, around every corner. Savoring the things right in front of you will give you a glimpse!

TO WRAP IT ALL UP, IN A PRETTY, PLEASANT-SMELLING PACKAGE...

Fulfillment in life comes as you learn to be your beautifully unique self.

So I think you get it now, but to sum it all up, every time you keep your SH** spreader from spewing all over, you are having a positive effect on something. Every time you do this, you're one step closer to becoming the person you were meant to be. The person you want to be. This leads you one step closer to being happy and fulfilled in life, bringing you closer to inner peace.

I'm not kidding. EVERY single time you stop and think before jumping in the SH** river, or adding to the SH** pile, you become more confident in who you are. Every time you make an effort to discourage someone else from doing the same, you're even closer.

Don't agree with every little view I have? Don't buy everything I say? That's awesome, because one of my priorities is to get people to stop and think for themselves and live by what they feel is right and best for them. Pay attention to what feels good to you, deep down, and you will know you are listening to your heart. PLEASE!!! Don't do things just because someone else is. Please.

My warmest wishes to you are that you discard the old habits that are not allowing you to grow and dream, and to form a new habit of stopping to think about what's best for you, regardless of what you have believed all these years. Any part of your past that does not serve you is meant to stay in the past. This includes any beliefs you have that are holding you back and not allowing what is best for you! I know that sounds rebellious, but how do you rebel against yourself? I'm sure the person that led you to believe what you do had only good intentions, but now that you're old enough to think for yourself, isn't it time to really firm up what helps you and what doesn't, and only move forward with what helps you? You are the only one that decides who you want to be. It's your life. You can make it whatever you want today. Today is a new day.

Now I'm not saying that your entire life will fall into place exactly as you want it to, now that you've read this marvelous book. No, your life is up to you, so what you do with the thinking this book might have started is up to you. Keep thinking, every minute of every day if you can, but otherwise, as much as possible! Realize that once you are someone you are proud of, you will notice that life will have many more options for you. You'll realize you can overcome anything, or at least go through it with dignity, and as someone people will look up to.

Read the sections on the topics you struggle with over and over, until you modify what you do into the way you want to think and the way you want to be. Think through what you are doing, whether you agree with my ideas or not. Practice thinking for yourself and before you know it, it will just happen automatically, all the time!

Be a positive influence to others and feel good about who you are. Be the person you have been yearning to be and really start enjoying your life. It's all yours and it's all up to you. No one else can be you, so just be you and smile lots! All you have to do is just start, and see how good it feels. Try it on for size now, and have a happy, fulfilling life. If you are a human being, you deserve that. And when people want to know what your secret is, just tell them to **RISE ABOVE THE SH**!**

298

TALK TO ME!

I would love to know what you think—about everything. I would love your feedback, your ideas, and especially, what other topics I could offer to help people? Please take the time to go to the publisher's website, ANNIEPRESS.COM, and follow the links to provide your valuable thoughts.

Also use ANNIEPRESS.COM to view more information on the author, the publisher, purchasing books, and how to contact us for anything you may need from us.

ANNIEPRESS.COM

302